# THE
# CHRISTMAS DAY
# MURDERS

**A True Crime Chronicle, Texas-style**

The Christmas Day Murders
A True Crime Chronicle, Texas-style

© 2007 J. B. Smith

Manufactured in the United States.

For information, please contact:
Brown Books Publishing Group
16200 North Dallas Parkway, Suite 170
Dallas, Texas 75248
www.brownbooks.com
972-381-0009
A New Era in Publishing™

ISBN-13: 978-1-933285-65-8
ISBN-10: 1-933285-65-6
LCCN: 2006907534
1 2 3 4 5 6 7 8 9 10

# THE CHRISTMAS DAY MURDERS

## A True Crime Chronicle, Texas-style

## Sheriff J. B. Smith
and
## D. W. Adams, Ph.D.

This book is dedicated to all my employees at the Smith County Sheriff's Office in Tyler, Texas. These men and women have allowed me to stand on their shoulders for almost thirty years. Their loyalty, dedication, perseverance, and downright love for the job make our agency stand out in this world of high-tech and basic "old shoe leather" murder investigations.

A special thanks goes to my wife, Vicki, for her patience when I was discouraged—and when the checks were written.

I also must give special thanks to my two sons, Danny and Robbie, for always believing in their old, reclusive, political dad when times were very rough.

Finally, thanks to the writer of this book, Dr. Dana Adams. He has dedicated his heart and soul to this endeavor. There is no way I could have accomplished this project without my "partner in crime."

Dana would like to thank his wife, Linda, and daughter-in-law, Cara, for their unrelenting belief that this book could be written, and to sons Trace and Brice for their encouragement as well.

# TABLE OF CONTENTS

## Part I
## MURDER IN SMITH COUNTY

# Part II
# THE INVESTIGATION

# Part III
# FEBRUARY: PRETRIAL EVENTS

*The Christmas Day Murders* is a journalistic account of the actual murder investigation of Stephanie Barron in 1999. The events recounted in this book are true; however, times and some names have been changed. The personalities, events, actions, and conversations portrayed in this book have been constructed using documents obtained through open records requests, personal interviews, trial transcripts, and press accounts.

# Part I
# MURDER IN SMITH COUNTY

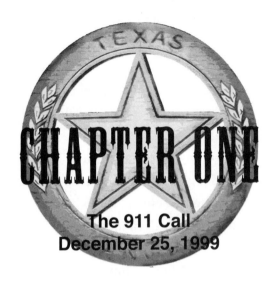

## CHAPTER ONE
### The 911 Call
### December 25, 1999

**4:20 a.m., Communications Center, Smith County Sheriff's Offices**

"Officer Tanner speaking. Do you need police, fire department, or emergency medical service?"

"Someone's broke into my granddaughter's house next door!"

"Ma'am, are you injured? What is your name and where are you calling from?"

"Someone's got a gun and they're shootin'!"

"Ma'am, please tell me your name. Are you injured?"

"Mrs. Toner. No, I'm not! Margaret Toner. I'm the grandmother. My husband and I live next door!"

"And where are you?"

"I'm at 11010 County Road 219, next to my daughter and

her family."

"Next door to who? Is that in Chapel Hill?"

"Yes. Get somebody over here! My granddaughter's scared to death, and so am I!"

"Yes, ma'am. You say you heard shots?"

"No, my granddaughter did. She saw someone that broke into the house, and her parents are still inside!"

"Ma'am, where is your granddaughter? Put her on the phone, please."

Communications Officer Pam Dunklin dispatches the sheriff's first response team to County Road 219, advising them that shots have been fired inside an occupied residence. Sergeant Pat Hendrix responds and says he is en route.

Senior Dispatcher Carolyn Tanner adjusts her headset as she scoots closer to the keyboard. It is time to confront the coming chaos. She quickly and expertly scans the five monitors in front of her, then focuses on monitor number two for the county map. She locates the source of the call in east Smith County, points, clicks, and drags to find the best route and the mileages. Then she checks monitor three, the unit assignment screen, to find the locations of the officers on patrol so she can continue pulling everything together.

She accomplishes all this while talking to Mrs. Toner. This is the ultimate in multitasking.

"Ma'am, please put your granddaughter on the phone now."

"Why? She's scared to death!"

Tanner uses her deepest voice and says sternly, "Ma'am."

"Here she is."

"What is your name?"

"Stephanie!" Her little-girl voice sounds out of breath from the excitement.

Sergeant Hendrix has been fielding complaints of fire-crackers going off. He thought that would probably be the extent of his calls early Christmas morning. The irony of it all—peace on earth and all that. But now his team will survey the scene and seal the area.

Dispatcher Dunklin notifies Emergency Medical Services to stage in the area, in case officers find gunshot victims. She listens to Dispatcher Tanner's conversation with the young girl.

"Stephanie, do you need medical attention?"

"No."

"Stephanie, tell me what happened."

"I heard four shots! Oh-my-god! They woke me up. I saw a shadow, but it was too dark. I hid in my closet with my phone, but it wouldn't work, so I ran over here to my grandmother's house."

"What is the address next door where you live, Stephanie?"

"11034 CR 219!" She still sounds a little out of breath. Tanner must keep her focused.

"Where did you see the shadow, the person?"

"Inside the house! Then I ran to my grandmother's. I didn't have time for shoes. I got sticker burrs in my feet."

"Are there any cars in the driveway?"

"Yeah, my mom's Buick and Dad's truck. There's another truck in the shed."

"Any strange vehicles, ones you don't recognize?"

"I didn't see any. It's pretty dark though."

Tanner tries to discern the girl's emotional state and lock the girl into a story. In the past, Tanner has talked people out of suicide or into confessing to a crime during the initial 911 call, so she asks as many questions as she can.

"What color are they?"

"The Buick is a blue Regal, and my dad's truck is black! They are still in there!"

"Your parents are in the house?"

"Yeah. Hey, I gotta hang up and check on them. Get somebody over here quick!"

"No, Stephanie. Stay on the line, stay with me. What are your parents' names?"

"Stephen and Carla Barron."

Officer Dunklin relays the information about the vehicles and the parents' names to the officers en route to the scene.

"Stay where you are Stephanie, hear me? Officers are on the way. Stay on the line with me. Did you hear or see any strange cars in the area?" Locking a caller into the story includes asking the same question to see if the answer is different the second time.

"No, ma'am."

"Any suspicious persons in the area today?"

"No."

Tanner asks Stephanie Barron to go over the events again in case she remembers something new that might be important or to see if she changes her story. The daughter begins, but what sounds to Tanner like dry heaves interrupts the seventeen-year-old's responses.

Dunklin's and Tanner's eyes meet at the sounds. Dunklin is new. She is a slender, attractive young woman; light brown hair with streaks of blond falls almost to her shoulders. Many women would pay lots of money for her sculptured nose. She has a little baby at home.

Tanner asks the daughter if she sees any sheriff's vehicles yet. Stephanie says that yes, they are here, and she drops the phone. Tanner disconnects reluctantly and reaches for her half-empty pack of cigarettes.

Tanner must know where her men are at all times. When they do not check in, she tracks them down. She feels a little nervous right now. The worst call for a dispatcher is to notify a deputy's wife when something terrible has happened to him. Finally Sergeant Hendrix calls and asks Tanner to phone the residence to see if anyone answers.

"Just the answering machine, sir."

7

"Damn it. OK, I'm goin' in."

A few moments later Hendrix advises Tanner of two deceased subjects inside the residence. Another tragedy on Christmas.

"Call Cox and Rasco. And the DA. Tell EMS to hold off. These victims are dead."

Tanner and Dunklin know the drill. One notifies Detectives Cecil Cox and Joe Rasco and relates that they are needed at a crime scene. The other contacts District Attorney Jack Skeen, who is always welcome at crime scenes. The DA's office offers valuable legal advice and generates search warrants. It is standard protocol to call him to the scene.

Tanner speaks: "Joe, sorry but you're not gonna believe this." Rasco always knows something is up by the sound of the dispatcher's voice. "We got a damn homicide on Christmas morning. Merry Christmas, by the way."

Dispatcher Tanner finally sips her warm Dr Pepper and thinks about going to peace officer's training school, the police academy, and becoming a certified Texas peace officer, so she can be out there where it happens. *Yeah, this is my last Christmas Eve on dispatch*, she thinks to herself.

The gregarious senior dispatcher, always with a ready quip and large, laughing eyes, has completed this shift many times because her kids are always at their father's for Christmas. She would be at home or at a bar with friends anyway. Calls about kids and suicides are the toughest. This time of year the number of suicide calls rises dramatically. Holidays can be terribly depressing for some people. Tanner remembers walking around for two weeks with her resignation in her back pocket because of the suicide calls. Her father is a retired cop in Kenner, Louisiana. He never quit and neither will she.

It feels as though since 4:30 a.m. everything has happened in slow motion. Tanner had been hoping for an easy shift with no lengthy follow-up reports. She updates her "Pass On" list for the next dispatcher, then calls her dad to tell him Merry Christmas.

All of Tanner's men will return to headquarters at some point during the next nine to twelve hours—all safe, she hopes.

# CHAPTER TWO

**Sheriff J. B. Smith**

Last Christmas morning, officers from my agency arrived around 4:30 a.m. at a crime scene in east Smith County. People say it's unnatural for parents to bury their children. This crime is even more unnatural than that—one I'll never forget. Two people were murdered while they were asleep on Christmas morning. Hell, there weren't even any presents to steal.

I'm J. B. Smith, a Texas sheriff. My agency investigated the tragic events surrounding the Barron murders, and as much we were fascinated with the actual time and the way these premeditated murders were committed, the 'why' of it all still lingers. There's a difference between a premeditated crime and a crime of passion. I'll save my thoughts on crimes of passion for another book.

The Barron capital murder case was settled before it went to trial because the defendant entered into a plea bargain. Part of the bargain was a confession. But sometimes I wonder about confessions as part of a plea bargain, which is an agreement between the state and the defendant. Each side gives up something and receives something in return. I realize it's an essential part of the legal process because if every criminal charge ended up in a trial, we'd be in a hell of a mess.

I am a student of human nature, and frankly, I'm spellbound by criminals' motives. Studying the criminal mind is one of the main things that keeps me on the job. And occasionally I have to help a friend who gets his butt in a crack, as we say in Texas.

Two of my main players on this particular case were Detective Joe Rasco, lead investigator, and Wade French, a licensed professional counselor and Ed.D. Rasco's extraordinary investigative work in accumulating and evaluating evidence and Dr. French's many insights into the mind of the psychopath contributed to bringing this case to an end.

My friend French has lots of experience in evaluating people charged with criminal acts. He began his career working in the state prison's maximum-security mental hospital. After spending time in juvenile probation, he worked with the federal probation system. During his sixteen years in the federal system, he was the chief United States probation officer. He's now in private practice and is one of the few mental-health professionals who has actually worked in the criminal justice system around here. From working in prisons as well as probation, he's got a very unique insight into criminal behavior. Although I've had my share of observing criminals, he's the expert and source for many of my comments on the psychopath,.

Although I'm not in the field as much as when I started in law enforcement on the West Coast, I wear a badge and carry a gun every day. Occasionally, I'll pull on my Western boots and hat. I admit I'm a cowboy at heart, but at first I didn't dress like it. I broke with a few traditions after I became the first Republican sheriff in the history of Smith County since its Reconstruction. Back in 1976, my opponents always wore white hats, white Western shirts, cowboy boots, and black-string ties. Now, there's nothing wrong with that here in Texas because that's the image. Hell, 1 percent of Texans still ride a horse to work. But I brought to the rodeo some new ideas in a pin-striped, three-piece suit. I wanted to bring Smith County out of the good-ole-boy mentality and into the age of technological crime detection with a new vocabulary, which I'm proud to say has been accomplished, by and large. Yes, there's still some of that back-slappin' stuff, but it's not like it used to be.

In my first campaign, I focused on crime and being the most experienced person to ever run for sheriff in Smith County. We're all concerned with violence in America, especially in our schools. It seems to me that too many kids don't care about the difference between right and wrong. I'm convinced that the Barron murders in Chapel Hill stemmed from gang-related activity of high-school-aged kids. Illegal drugs and weapons were involved, as usual.

The terrible events that unfolded in Littleton, Colorado, at Columbine High School constantly remind us what can happen in our schools. I recall several other incidents in the late nineties that received national attention. In June 1999, I read another report on violence. America ranked third behind Mexico and Russia.

Smith County has more than its share of homicides per square mile and per capita. Homicide is a peculiar type of crime that's different from the natural death of a ninety-year-old grandparent quietly passing away. It's the unnaturalness of murder that seems so foreign, so intrusive, and so evil to right-minded people.

A crime scene that involves a homicide, or several, never gets any easier to understand. I'm told that the United States Senate is the most exclusive club in the world. My club is pretty damn exclusive too—the world of unnatural death, most aptly put, is "a world that begins when yours ends."

As sheriff of Smith County, I'm responsible for all homicide investigations. My chief deputy and I direct fifteen detectives in the criminal investigation division and another seventy-five patrol personnel who work the county. A day-sergeant and a night-sergeant handle those on patrol. A third sergeant is in charge of drugs. I keep around two hundred deputies working the jail. They're all deputies and certified peace officers in the state of Texas. Every now and then I call up the reserves, about twenty or so. This has been my job since 1977. I do it for a living because I care about this county and the people here. That's why my staff attend the best schools in the nation for up-to-date technology and information. That way I can surround myself with intelligent people who know what they're doing. That's what Teddy Roosevelt believed: surround yourself with the right people and the rest will take care of itself.

My headquarters are in a sixteen-story white building located one block south of the Smith County Courthouse, on the town square. The building used to be the Carlton Hotel, built in 1954, and noted for the swimming pool at the top and the parties in the ballroom. It also featured a radio in all two hundred rooms and a television in every suite. I'm told it was really something.

I think we should all be interested in local history. For example, my parking garage on the east side of headquarters was built over deep natural springs. Big-ass, heavy-duty jacks were brought in from the coast to find suitable bedrock for the structure. They dug deep and finally succeeded. That's why the street running north along the east side of the square is called Spring Street.

The Smith County Jail opened in 1985. People around here

don't seem to understand that the population of the jail has doubled every ten years for the past thirty years. It ain't my fault. Criminals got to be somewhere other than on the streets of Smith County.

The headquarters now house the Precinct One Justice, the constable, four fire marshals, the probation department, and the district attorney's offices. My agency occupies floors one, two, five, six, seven, and sixteen.

Another thing people don't understand is that crime investigation is not television drama. Crimes are not solved quickly and neatly at the end of sixty minutes. It often takes months to build a case for prosecution and more time for the trial. The Barron double-murder case nearly went to trial, but at the last minute, Detective Joe Rasco produced some irrefutable evidence that changed everything. The defense attorneys knew they were hog-tied, so they advised their client to plea out, as we say. I guess Rasco's last-minute heroics sound like television drama. But that's what happened.

# CHAPTER THREE

## Rasco's Trip to the Crime Scene

If asked, Detective Joe Rasco will say he is not from anywhere. People who grow up in military families often have vague memories of small houses on military base after military base. The houses look the same; everything runs together.

Joe Rasco is an articulate, reserved man. The kind who speaks only when he has something relevant to say. A well-traveled, well-educated person, he knows how to conjugate irregular verbs correctly when he talks. Rasco reads a lot; he is not from around here.

Rasco appreciates the value of words and reads mainly nonfiction. He cannot find anything more exciting and bizarre than in the newspaper. Hawthorne, Poe, and Melville took newspaper headlines and shaped stories from them. Rasco briefly taught American literature in high school after he retired from the Air Force, but it was not for him. Not enough discipline in the school systems.

Detective Rasco's trim, 5'10" build is not overly muscular for his height. His short, cropped hair shows a little gray. He wears the standard gray, long-sleeved polo shirt with the sheriff's department logo; tactical 5-11 black combat pants; black, boot-type, high-top shoes; and a bomber jacket, much like the one he wore in the Air Force. His weapon, a Glock .40-caliber semiautomatic, hangs at his waist. To the left of his belt buckle is his badge. His bullet-proof vest stays in his black Crown Victoria; the car is always full of gas for times like this when nothing is open.

This is Rasco's third homicide case with Sheriff J. B. Smith. After only weeks in the detective division, Rasco sees similarities to his twenty-six years as an Air Force lieutenant colonel. The six thousand hours of flight time in jets and C-130 four-engine turbo-prop cargo transports have given him the patience, self-discipline, and attention to detail that investigative work demands. He is a former flight instructor; his father is retired Air Force too. His background is ideal for his current profession. After all, a detective's job is somewhat para-military in scope with mission mentality.

As Joe leaves his dark house, the only light comes from the Christmas tree reflecting off the shiny packages. His wife always prepares the decorations, and they are beautiful as usual. It is a tradition to leave the tree lights on for Christmas Eve. *Too many presents. We've got to cut back. But I think I said that last year*, Joe muses as he shuts the door behind him.

The early-morning phone call sends Joe directly into protocol, or target fixation, as they call it in the military. Rasco slides into the Crown Vic. He likes the handling and performance package: 200 horsepower, dual exhausts, and a specially designed suspension. As the sixteen-valve, V-8, Police Interceptor engine fires, Rasco's mind shifts into gear with a pre-flight checklist: photographs, fingerprinting, evidence collection, witness interviews. He will discern the type and cause of death: natural, suicide, homicide, or a combination. He may need a signed consent-to-search form from the daughter.

The one thing Rasco can count on is that there is never an ideal crime scene. The rules cannot be stressed enough at a crime scene: unless injured victims need immediate medical attention, nobody touches a damn thing until detectives assess the scene. The investigation team cannot allow a scene to be compromised in any way: no emergency medical technicians, no over-eager reporters, no gawking neighbors, no off-duty law enforcement dropping by to see some blood and guts. Protecting the scene from contamination is paramount. Rasco remembers a long-time senior officer known for smoking at crime scenes. Rasco wanted to kick his butt into the next county. That officer is no longer with the agency.

Protocol: if a victim is dying, get a deathbed statement. The guidelines for that are very specific. The person making the deathbed statement must know that he is dying and must die. Otherwise, what a person says could be considered hearsay and would not be admissible in court. The idea is that a dying person has no reason to lie.

Another rule is that evidence is in the details, not in memory. Everything must be written down. Cases are won and lost on details. Even witnesses cannot rely on their memories, and a good prosecution lawyer will rip a witness's head off and hand it back to him if he fails to answer questions confidently and accurately while on the witness stand.

Yet another rule: witnesses must be isolated from each other immediately to avoid a joint story of the events that the perpetrators have agreed upon.

Rasco hopes everything is pristine as he works his way into the Barron crime area. All he knows is that there is a house and a murder. He drives to Chapel Hill from his home in Flint, a small community in south Smith County.

The morning is cold and clear—low 40s. The twenty-five-minute drive is uneventful except for two things: everything is dark and closed for the holiday. Rasco does not see a single car all the way to Chapel Hill. It is as if the rest of the human race disappeared during the night, and he is the only one left. As he leaves the rural community behind, he notices few street-lights or Christmas lights. He meets a wall of towering, dark pine trees as he stops and turns east toward Old Jacksonville

Highway. Five miles to go until he reaches Loop 323, which encircles Tyler. He pauses at the intersection of the four-way stop in Gresham, another small community in south Smith County. Rasco says out loud, "One of these drives, I'm going to count the number of churches on this road." Whatever turns these folks on is fine with him. East Texas is known for its religiosity. Many of the congregations are nondenominational, Pentacostal, or fundamental. They live in their gardens of Eden and fear the devil's temptations; Satan stalks them day and night.

**4:45 a.m.**

Sergeant Pat Hendrix is the first on the scene. With gun drawn, he moves slowly toward the back door, which is cracked open. He pushes it wider and yells, "Sheriff's office!" twice before stepping inside. Hendrix does not need a consent to search the residence. He proceeds to conduct a welfare check on possible gunshot victims who might need immediate medical attention. He might even find a murderer inside. He enters through a utility room. A night light shines from a wall in the bathroom. Hendrix continues to another room where the door is slightly ajar. He nudges it open with his flashlight and sees a body on the bed highlighted by the brightness of the beam. Then another body on the floor.

**4:54 a.m.**

Detective Rasco turns right on the Loop. The strange, dark nothingness continues. He passes gas stations, Chili's, and TGIF and cruises silently through the busiest intersection in the city. He is the only moving object. He slows at the huge Troup Highway intersection and drives on toward Old Henderson Highway, which will take him to Chapel Hill and County Road 219 to the Barrons' home.

The turn south onto CR 219 is at the corner "Stop and Rob," as officers call it, because of the many times burglars hit it. The county road is a two-lane, close oil-topped road with a long dip in it about halfway to the crime scene, over a mile away from the Stop and Rob. The dip is hard to see with all the tall trees, but the moonlight drifts easily out of the winter foliage and reflects on the road. To Rasco's left is the Oil Palace, a monstrous, domed building built by the Manziel family to exhibit top-flight boxing matches. Jack Dempsey's good friend and sparring partner decades ago, Mr. Manziel, loved boxing. Former local heavyweight boxer Buddy Turman added to Tyler's renown for producing great boxers. Some people in town claim he was one of the best heavyweights in the world. He matched gloves with Floyd Patterson and Archie Moore. Turman's record was 45-15-2, with 32 knockouts before he retired from the ring in 1967.

**4:58 a.m.**

Detective Rasco turns through the simple iron gate, hedged

on either side by wild bushes, It is the only way in. He sees a dim light seeping from narrow, rectangular-shaped windows on the left and right sides of the house. A kitchen light shines from the grandparents' house next door. Rasco reaches for his notebook on the front seat.

He stops behind a black GMC extended cab pickup parked under a large tree just to the east of the house. Condensation covers the vehicle. Walking toward the truck, Rasco sees a cooler in the bed containing ice and several Natural Light beers. As he circles the truck, he notes that there are no breaks in the condensation. The tailgate is down. Two empty beer cans perch on it.

Rasco smells smoke. It reminds him of a campfire. Walking a few feet to the west, he finds a Buick Regal. No breaks in the dew on this vehicle either. A quick peek reveals that the cellular phone has been turned off. Nothing remarkable.

In the old days, the gumshoe cops damaged too much potential evidence. "You can't just go balls-to-the-walls up to a crime scene," the sheriff had told Rasco the first day on the job. Sheriff Smith sends his people to schools that stress the technological side of investigations. Rasco recently graduated from a weapons and ballistics institute and a fingerprint school conducted by the FBI.

Christmas. *Why the hell would anyone murder someone on Christmas morning? You just don't think things like this happen in Tyler,* Rasco thinks. But Tyler is becoming more and more cosmopolitan, despite the conservative population, and sometimes that kind of growth is costly. The bankers, the realtors, and the chamber of commerce love it, but so much building activity can attract the wrong kind of people. To keep costs at a minimum, employers hire illegal migrant workers and pay them next to nothing. Most are good, hard-working laborers, but a small number of them work labor jobs during the day and commit crimes at night. They just cannot make a living working for so little. That said, no circumstance, economic or otherwise, allows for condoning crime. Rasco is a pragmatist when it comes to the law.

He continues his walk around the outside of the house trailer and finds a small garage attached to the southwest corner. Inside the garage is a new, red Dodge Ram pickup. It is locked.

**5:11 a.m.**

Sergeant Hendrix, crime-scene supervisor and one of the "midnight sergeants," gives Rasco the rudimentary information. "Two adults in the master bedroom, both shot. There's a girl next door—looks like she can't be more than twelve. She ran over to her grandmother's house after she heard shots. She's still in her pajamas. Says she heard footsteps in her bedroom but no voices. She was hiding in her closet. Says her parents are the ones in the house."

More deputies arrive. One says to Rasco, "That little girl

next door says she run out of here so fast she didn't put on her clothes. Wants to know can she dress now?"

The detective winces; the deputy failed to conjugate an irregular verb correctly, something Rasco has grown accustomed to, unfortunately. It is hard not to be a pedant. "No, she cannot."

He turns to Sergeant Hendrix. "Is that about it?"

"So far. I found the back door slightly ajar when I entered the residence in the initial search. No one inside except the victims. I checked the pulses, but that's all I touched."

"Let's go through the crime scene."

They walk through the back entrance into the washroom that leads to the kitchen. There is just enough light coming from the other end of the mobile home to see the main living area. Rasco keeps his hands behind his back or in his pockets so he will not inadvertently touch anything.

"Something's odd here besides a killing," Rasco mutters.

Hendrix quickly concurs, "Weird."

"No Christmas tree."

"Yeah. No presents either."

Detective Rasco's thoughts turn briefly to his waiting family. His son and daughter-in-law are in town for a traditional holiday: lots of presents on Christmas morning, a large, well-ornamented tree in the foyer, and a big family dinner on Christmas Eve. Each person opens one present after dinner, a tradition started by his father-in-law many years ago when

Joe's kids were little. But now his son is a police officer in Richardson, just north of Dallas. The family understands. Everyone will wait for Santa Claus, but he will not arrive until eleven o' clock Christmas night.

As Rasco moves toward the master bedroom and into the stark light, he sees a female on the bed. Her pale skin shows a bluish tint. The bedspread covers her almost to the neck. Except for the bullet hole under her left eye, she looks as though she is sleeping peacefully. The blood from the gunshot wound does not quite match the pink roses on the bedspread and makes her white t-shirt look tie-dyed. He sees blood under the right arm too, the arm that cradles a small, long-haired Scottish terrier. A Chihuahua sits quietly by the victim's head. The dogs refuse to move, which is good because they would spread blood everywhere and complicate the scene. Rasco would like to think that they have not moved since the shooting, but he realizes this is a lot to hope for.

Another body on the floor leans against the bed, his face cushioned by the mattress. The overweight victim is in his underwear. Since Smith County does not have a medical examiner or coroner, the bodies will be sent to the Southwest Institute of Forensic Science after a justice of the peace pronounces them dead. A trickle of blood runs down the front of the body. Half-open eyes peer up from a bearded face; the right arm rests partially on the blood-soaked bed. The hands are not clutching anything, and both arms and hands look relaxed. Rasco speculates that there was no struggle, because when the muscles are tight at the moment of death, cadaveric spasm usually sets in. The left leg is bent, foot under crotch. The right leg stretches out covering brown house shoes—moccasins that match his wife's. He looks as though he rolled out of bed. Behind him, an eight-by-ten, framed color photo of his smiling daughter sits on the nightstand.

Hendrix gestures toward the man. "Could be what you'll find here, Joe, is a murder-suicide."

Rasco does not respond.

"You'll probably find a gun under that pillow or under the male."

Based on a first look, the idea seems reasonable to Rasco. Husband shoots her, then himself. A domestic struggle. Happens all the time.

Rasco says, "They certainly didn't argue over Christmas presents. If it's armed robbery, they took the tree along with the presents."

People have been killing each other since the beginning of time. Punishable by death, capital murder appears in an early chapter of Genesis in the Hebrew text. In England during the eighteenth century, some 240 crimes were punishable by death. Causing the death of another person without legal justification such as self-defense, defense of property, or law enforcement, is murder.

Rasco moves closer. "I can feel it. You ever felt or smelled death, Sergeant?"

"Yeah. I'm afraid so. Unholy."

"Well, she's been shot at least once in the face, looks like. Arm too." Rasco walks around the bed for a better look at the male, reaches out, and straightens the head back slightly. "He's got at least one wound to the back of the head. That doesn't make sense. There must have been another person, the shooter, probably standing on her side of the bed near the doorway."

Rasco surmises that the shooter killed the woman first and then shot the man, who tried to escape after suddenly waking up. He never had a chance. "Double homicide," announces Detective Rasco, "which will make the charge capital murder."

"The man is obviously familiar with weapons," continues Rasco. "He might have tried to reach under the bed for a gun when he heard shots. I don't see any defensive wounds on either body—no struggle. I saw an empty leather holster and an open box of Remington-Peters in the washroom as we came in. Looks like .35-caliber. Must be forty-five or fifty live rounds. Look at that." Rasco points across the room. "A bullet hole in the window. There's a nick here on the headboard. The shooter missed at least once. Maybe twice."

He thanks the sergeant. "I'll take it from here." Hendrix is proud of Rasco; Hendrix trained him.

Rasco pulls a small lockbox out from under the bed.

Inside he finds a .25-caliber semiautomatic pistol and a black 9 mm Beretta in a camouflage, cloth pouch with a magazine containing four live rounds. He reaches farther under the bed and discovers a Brown North American Arms gun case with a .22-caliber five-shot revolver inside. "This guy wasn't planning on taking crap from anyone, that's for sure, but somebody took him by surprise. I'll bet there are weapons in his truck too."

"I'll go check." Hendrix inspects the black pickup in the driveway, finding a white cotton sock in the console that contains a black steel Grendel .380 model P12 loaded with ten rounds of Remington-Peters bullets. No bullet in the chamber. Easily visible in the console area is $200 and change. The murderer either did not see the cash or did not care.

Investigator Rasco slowly surveys the rest of the trailer's interior. Just off the master bedroom, he sees matching sinks and closets on either side of the bathtub. A toilet is next to one sink, a shower next to the other.

He moves through the living room and office area, which would appear normal on any day other than Christmas. Everything is in order; nothing is damaged. A new computer, sewing machine, jambox, and small television are all in their place. The drawers are not pulled out in the master bedroom enough to be relevant.

*Doesn't appear to be robbery*, he notes to himself.

He walks down a short hallway to the other entrance—still locked—and finds the daughter's room in the northwest corner of the trailer. It looks like a typical teenager's bedroom. It is messy but not ransacked, clothes everywhere, unmade bed. He checks the caller ID and writes in his notebook the phone number of a call that came in at 1:31 a.m.

Returning to the master bedroom area, Rasco finds a man's leather wallet with a driver's license, a Texas concealed handgun license number 0179159, credit cards issued to Stephen Barron, and $255 in cash. From the evidence found in the truck and in the house, the case looks less and less like a robbery. On the woman's side of the bedroom, he finds a pocketbook belonging to Carla Barron with identification and $140. More than $400 inside the residence that the shooter did not steal.

Before he inventories the outside, Rasco runs another mental checklist. In any homicide investigation, a critical step toward solving a crime is to get everyone—surviving victims, witnesses, and suspects—locked into their story right away; so if there is some divergence from that story later, it can be contrasted with the original documentation. Dispatcher Tanner started that process during the 911 call. In conjunction with evidence, the goal of the investigation is to blow holes through testimony and turn an actual witness or an observer into a possible suspect.

Rasco turns and moves slowly toward the back entrance to make his way out. The dogs are still on the bed with their owners. He does not want to startle them.

# CHAPTER FOUR

## September:
## People Are Strange

As the sheriff, I spend time at my small ranch thinking about what's going on in Smith County—all 933 square miles and almost 200,000 people. I sip a little Crown Royal and Coke or vodka and orange juice here in my log home. A lot goes on in this big county—everything from the personal problems of 281 employees to budget meetings with the commissioners' court to homicide investigations.

I like to study people. But as soon as I think I've got a grip on human nature, something crazy like this double homicide happens on Christmas morning, and I feel like I've been bitten in the butt. That's an interesting word—*crazy*. The criminal mind is fascinating because not all criminals are considered crazy or criminally insane. It never made any sense to me until Dr. Wade French and I started our many discussions on psychopaths.

When it comes to a double murder on Christmas morning, well, that's the kind of thing that holds my attention for a very long time. We solved the case in due course with diligent detective work and crime lab evidence; although there was another important player who could very well have been much more involved than we proved, he wound up in the pen on other charges.

According to statements made by their friends, Stephen and Carla Barron seemed to be pretty normal folks. Mr. Barron worked in Dallas, and Mrs. Barron stayed at home. At the time of the murders, Carla was recuperating from brain surgery. They had one daughter, Stephanie.

Chapel Hill sits east of Tyler on your way to Henderson. From Henderson, you used to go around one of those traffic circles and come out going north to the Red River, east to Louisiana, or south to deep East Texas toward the Big Thicket and on to the Gulf.

East Texas people are independent. Matter of fact, in 1870, many people here supported the idea of creating another state in East Texas. People are a little different around these parts, especially the farther you go toward the Big Thicket swamps. In 1898, a bunch of wide-eyed patriots organized the Fourth Texas Volunteer Infantry and called themselves the "Smith County Rifles." Off they galloped to serve in the Spanish-American War, but I'm told they never saw any action.

Sometimes the people here take the law into their own hands. I recall reading about a lynching that occurred in 1909. At the time, the county was building a new courthouse, and a mob took over the hoisting equipment used in the construction and hung the guy. This was pretty rough territory in the old days.

Although September began slowly at my office, it was a strange month. The first day of the month was the hottest day of the year, around 105 degrees as I recall. And two months without rain set another record.

With everything around here as brittle as a dead leaf, area fire departments responded to over a hundred fires in Smith County in September, another record. Lordy, it was weird. Seven fires in one day, as I remember. One in Chapel Hill off County Road 26 about nine miles east of here. The newspaper said a pine tree caught fire and exploded. Went straight up in the air 'bout twenty feet like a damn rocket.

My little spread, as we say in Texas, is about twenty-five minutes from Tyler. It's in a little place called Starrville, not more than a few houses, a community center we still use, and the original Starrville Colored Christian Methodist Episcopal Church, established in 1870. Yep, that's what they named it. I guess they didn't want to leave anybody out. Starrville is an example of fate or bad luck, depending on how you see it. When the road from Georgia came through Starrville and went all the way to California, Starrville was larger than Tyler.

But the railroad changed all that when it was built closer to Tyler.

Don't get me wrong. I like it in East Texas. Everybody leaves you alone unless you're in politics. That's one reason I live here in Starrville. People ask me what I raise on my spread. I always say my major crops are coyotes, armadillos, and fire ants.

From where I'm sitting right now, I can see for about fifty miles all the way to Titus County. I'm an official weather observer for the National Weather Service in Shreveport. When it rains, I call them. One night I saw lightning in the north, so I checked in with Shreveport. They said the lightning was about fifty-five miles from where I was sitting. From my back porch I can see Wood County and the lights in Big Sandy in Upshur County and the lights from Gladewater in Gregg County. When I retire as sheriff, you won't be able to budge me from this lounge chair. It's been broken many times, but I always fix it because I can't bear to part with it. When I'm on the back porch, what I listen for is that lonesome train whistle coming from Big Sandy.

September is the beginning of football season, and all of the towns in Smith County, large and small, have a team. I can't tell you how much people love their high-school teams around here. Signs go up everywhere; store owners write slogans in their front windows; brightly dressed cheerleaders with permanent smiles dance everywhere with their ponytails flapping the backs of their necks. Around here, school spirit is something to behold.

It's all pretty high-stakes stuff. But it seems to me that sports can reflect the unruly elements in our society. It's so violent, predatory, and vengeful—especially in the pro leagues. I see more and more violent people in and out of sports without a hint of a conscience. After a player puts his opponent in the hospital, he doesn't have any remorse. I believe that kind of mentality is antisocial.

Dr. French has studied violent children who grow into adult killers and never consider themselves wrong because they believe their victims deserved to die. They feel they did the victims a favor by killing them. Sometimes killers think they are the victims, but they stalk the emotionally weak and vulnerable. That's what sports do: identify the weaknesses of an opponent and attack them. In the process, somebody goes to the emergency room with a broken neck. In the Barron case, Stephanie considered herself a victim of strict parents because they grounded her for her rebellious behavior, her hot checks, and a forgery charge. Her father was the enforcer, but her mother was sympathetic. I think Stephanie preyed on the sympathies and weaknesses of her mother. From what I can tell, the family situation was producing a lot of stress.

When I grew up, hell, we didn't know what stress was. Life was simple. I'm the son of a sharecropping family. Many of us worked at the local sawmill or picked cotton. Simply existing and feeding ourselves was a struggle. I had five brothers and sisters, and my step-daddy was an alcoholic. I never knew my real father. We had a pretty hard life, but we didn't know it because everyone else was just like us. I remember stuffing newspapers into knotholes in the wall and floor to keep the cold out. In the wintertime, ice formed around the knotholes in the floor. I quit school in the eighth grade to pick cotton to the tune of one dollar for a hundred pounds. Five days of picking cotton bought one pair of Levi's. Life was pretty hard back in Arkansas, but now I enjoy driving back to see my brothers and sister.

I'm a long way from Arkansas in many ways. Matter of fact, I consider roughin' it a motel without room service or camping in an air-conditioned Winnebago. I don't mind saying I'm an uncomplicated man, although I do have a B.S. in criminal justice from the University of Texas at Tyler. I earned that degree by going to school at night. I'm a very hard and determined worker because I grew up knowing the value of work. Not because I wanted to, mind you, but because I had to. I am smart enough to surround myself with intelligent employees, associates, and friends, and they have helped me become successful as sheriff. I help them too. At some time or another, it seems that everybody needs something from their sheriff.

Everyone around here knows Red Little. He's needed a little help more than once. Red's done very well in the insurance business for over fifty years. He bought an insurance agency in Rusk in 1954 and moved it to Tyler.

Red and I don't have lots of degrees, and we both rode a plow mule from the fields when we were young. But we make up for all that with a positive attitude and hard work.

Here's another thing Red and I agree on: we love the women. On a couple of occasions he's called me for help from a closet in a young woman's bedroom. The husband came home a little early.

Once he flew some ladies-of-the-evening down here from New York. I didn't know who else was involved, but Red apparently had quite a time. One of the women stole his solid-gold Rolex. He called me, and I intercepted her at the airport and took her off the plane. She and I had a short, "Come to Jesus Meeting," as I call it. Let's just say Red got his watch back. Years later he gave me the watch. No words were needed. Close friendships are like that.

My friend Dr. Wade French and I go back several years. He encouraged me when I was going through some hard times, and I've done the same for him. French tells me that for some people, violence may be dictated by the brain. Of course, we don't know for sure if violence is caused by nature and genetics or nurture and environment, but from my years of experience observing criminals, I'm inclined to say it is more genes and the way a predator's brain works than anything else. I'm told that a psychopath's brain may grow at an abnormally slow pace.

Dr. French says that adult EEGs of psychopaths are similar to teenagers, so some adults often never fully develop.

A professor friend of mine at the University of Texas at Tyler says we are hardwired with the structures of our native grammar before we're born. At a very young age, children use grammar before they ever receive any instruction, regardless of the language.

It could be that the psychopath comes into this world wired differently that normal people. All the wires aren't connected, especially in the front part of the brain, which has a lot to do with behavior. They are born with these misconnections, and that's why I think a large part of the psychopath's problems are related to the brain and to genes. The elevator skips a floor every now and then on the way to the top, if you get my drift.

Some kids turn out all right regardless of their environment. But not all of them. As kids grow older, they become more cunning and manipulative if they have psychopathic tendencies. Sometimes there's a trigger that sets them off, but it could be that the mind set is already in place because of a genetic predisposition.

There are things we as reasonable human beings don't understand. For example, the figures I've seen tell me that some of these abnormal kids come from stable families. The psychotic predisposition may solve the mystery of why, in spite of a stable and nurturing environment, some children

become damned ornery and end up as violent career criminals. That's one of the theories we initially worked with in
the Barron case: normal parents, abnormal child. An event
triggers psychotic behavior, and the event can be something
as simple as grounding a young person for disobeying. That
social restriction becomes a huge ordeal in a psychopath's
mind.

Psychopaths come in all shapes and sizes. Some are smart,
some are dumb, and some are average in intelligence. Male
psychopaths outnumber female psychopaths five to one.
Regardless of gender or intelligence, French says they all
have the same personality characteristics that set them apart.
They are pathologically self-centered, have little or no ability
to experience true guilt or remorse, and can't control their
impulses. By and large, I'd say that human behavior is regulated
by inhibition. Guilt, remorse, and fear of rejection inhibit most
people from acting on their unacceptable impulses, wishes, or
fantasies. So without the ability to experience these inhibiting
emotions, the psychopath acts on the most diabolic impulses.
Hell, some of them think they're smarter than the rest of us
and are immune from punishment. And that ain't so.

We catch them, they get out, and they commit another crime
because they have no remorse whatsoever. Society likes to
blame everything on drugs, and I'm certainly not denying that
particular problem, but the tap root of a psychopath is their
predatory nature; that's the most important factor, it seems

to me. You can take away the drugs, but you can't take away the evil behavior of a psychopath once they follow that path, because drugs are not the source of the problem. They are a byproduct. What scares the holy crap outta me is that we have a large segment of the population classified as psychopathic in varying degrees. Dr. French tells me that some 20 percent of the prison population is psychopathic. They commit probably as many as half of all crimes.

French has much experience in evaluating this type of behavior. He and I agree that the issue with psychopaths is not treatment and rehabilitation, it's protecting the public from harm and managing those people interested only in satisfying their own needs. That usually means sending them to the pen so they can't exploit or harm others. While many young people show mild to moderate antisocial behavior into early adulthood, most eventually mature out of these self-defeating behaviors, usually by the time they are thirty. Not so with a psychopath. They will scheme, connive, and exploit others until the day they die.

Incarceration rarely solves the problem. I know, because I run one of the largest county jails in the country with over a thousand in daily population. I see them come and go with a 72 percent recidivism rate. And that's unacceptable to my way of thinking.

# CHAPTER FIVE

## "I Love Money"

**5:40 a.m.**

In another life, Detective Joe Rasco was probably an artist. He enjoys sketching for pleasure. But this is business. He takes his pencil, marks north, south, east, and west, then draws a schematic of the crime scene in his notebook for the case file. As he waits for the other members of the crime investigation team, who are just arriving, he marks the dimensions of the trailer home and blocks in all the rooms in his drawing, carefully detailing the main objects—chairs, desks, beds. Someone else can measure it accurately later. While it is fresh on his mind, and before EMS is involved, he draws an exploded view of the bedroom, noting details such as holes in the window, chips in the headboard possibly from a gunshot, and position of the bodies. The finished drawing will be completed at his office on his computer.

Because bodies are only in the bedroom, he makes no sketch of the outside after he leaves the trailer. Everything glistens in the early-morning dew: the black pickup, the patrol cars. Christmas morning dawns chilly as the sun creeps up.

### 5:58 a.m.

Detective Cox arrives after retrieving the mobile crime scene unit from the sheriff's office downtown. He sees that the patrol division has secured the area. The mobile unit, dubbed "Snoopy," houses a stunning array of evidence-gathering and assimilating equipment. "Snoopy" has everything from the standard fingerprinting kits to trace metal and military survival kits. Photography equipment includes 35 mm SLR cameras, 300 mm zoom and 28-135 mm wide-angle lenses, tripods, flash attachments, a video camera, and a Polaroid camera. And of course, a Coleman 3500-watt generator. Sledge hammers, pry bars, bolt cutters, machetes, and metal detectors hang ready for use.

The Smith County Sheriff's Agency uses the premier crime scene unit in this part of the state, along with more firepower than some small countries. The sheriff commands a small army of cavalry and armored personnel carriers. The mounted horse patrol, along with a well-respected tracking dog unit, handles crowd control, and both are often used in other areas of Texas. The United States Army surplus armored personnel carriers, named Bubba I and Bubba II, will quiet a hostile crowd just by showing up. Bubba I has a smiley face with the slogan "Have a Nice Day" on the back.

Evidence-gathering techniques improve every year. The value of early retrieval of evidence is inestimable. Scientific DNA matches exert much sway in courtrooms because jurors have become well versed in crime detection and techniques from watching television. They expect it. However, DNA gathered at a murder scene does not guarantee identification because of the lack of matching information from available records. Smith County has access to the computerized, national DNA database in Gregg County. The database was developed and is maintained by the FBI. Although it is far from comprehensive, it is a start.

Cox steps down from the unit and acknowledges Rasco, along with other officers at the scene. "Merry Christmas."

"Screw you," Rasco quips.

Detective Cecil Cox and FBI Special Agent Jeff Millslagle walk the short distance toward Rasco, who stands at the west side of the home in deep shadows. They survey the entire scene.

The early light reveals that the Barron home is a modest residence, a white, double-wide mobile home with blue trim and an attached garage. A large satellite dish, about sixty feet away, gapes upward and to the south. Rasco steps up to the narrow rear porch and patio area. On the back porch, which extends the length of the mobile home, sits a refrigerator/ freezer just to the left of the back door. He routinely checks the door for evidence of forced entry. There are the usual lawn chairs separated by a white plastic table with an empty ceramic bowl on top. A brown ice chest and a blue cooler rest next to each other across from the barbecue pit. Wind chimes hang silently. Nothing is growing from the wooden, iron-ribbed cask just to the right of the steps. The clock on the outside wall has stopped. *Things are as they should be on the outside*, he supposes.

The investigators, arms behind backs, stand a few feet away from the home. Rasco sees the daughter's bedroom on the corner of the residence, where she apparently slept until she heard shots. Rasco knows the difference between using the words *apparently* and *evidently*. They are not interchangeable. If her story is factual and true, he will use the word *evidently*, but not until then. Cox crosses his arms over his chest and scans the entire mobile home. "So the parents died in their bedroom on the opposite end of the house?"

"Evidently." Rasco notices the small bedroom windows, a tight squeeze for a person to crawl inside. Millslagle notes that the kitchen light is on at the grandmother's house next door. Mr. and Mrs. Toner live in a brick home with white columns supporting a small front porch. Inside, the granddaughter writes a statement. She is an attractive, polite, diminutive girl with a light complexion and long, brown hair. She stresses that she heard someone in the house. The dogs will not shut up now, but the daughter fails to mention any barking in her statement. Apparently the gunshots woke her, not the dogs outside her window.

At the northeast corner of the property, a telephone pole is linked by wires and cable to the Barron residence. Lead Detective Rasco walks to the electrical box and makes a note of the mangled wires. Someone tried to cut the smaller wires attached to the house. He turns to the others. "Whoever tried this was not very successful. Or smart. The phones still work."

**6:29 a.m.**

"Hey, Joe! Come 'ere! I found something!" Special Agent Jeff Millslagle, a transfer from Dallas, is a member of Tyler's FBI office and a part of the Smith County Violent Crimes Task Force. He has been with the Bureau for fourteen years and is highly trained in investigating bank robberies and kidnapping; in gathering counter-intelligence; in collecting, identifying, and packaging physical evidence; and in the two relatively new areas of computer crime and identity theft. Detective Cecil Cox carefully places samples collected from the bathroom into a medium-sized plastic bag with a preprinted evidence tag. All Smith County detectives are familiar with the standard evidence collection kit: pharmacy-type vials, airtight plastic containers, rubber gloves, tweezers, and small paper envelopes—the kind a coin collector might use. Physical evidence includes any type of material that can be seen or measured.

Detective Joe Rasco grabs his camera from the dresser in the master bedroom. Cox and Rasco are the only two people designated to collect evidence; they move briskly through the office area separating the two bedrooms toward a small closet at the other end of the mobile home. Rasco arrives first.

"Looks like a .38." Agent Millslagle crouches on one knee as he carefully pushes some clothes aside in the corner of the closet. The agent is dressed for the occasion: black mock turtleneck with the Federal Bureau of Investigation insignia on the left, khaki cargo pants with deep pockets, and leather, ankle-high boots. His jacket is the usual lined, black Windbreaker with the letters F-B-I in yellow on the back. He is a slender man with light, receding hair, about the same size as Rasco. The agent has an inquisitive manner—eyes always alert.

"Wooden grips. Looks like a blue-steel, five-shot revolver," Rasco observes. "Where exactly was it?"

"Inside the front pocket of this sweatshirt. I didn't take it out, just noticed the sweatshirt was too heavy when I checked underneath it. So I looked inside."

"Damn good thing it doesn't have a hair trigger."

"Son of a bitch."

Rasco expertly handles the weapon. He does not jab a pencil

down the barrel TV-style. That could ruin evidence. The inside grooves and the twisting pattern a bullet makes on firing are critical in matching bullets. He pokes his pen through the trigger guard and behind the trigger, then slowly raises it to eye level. "It's not fully loaded. A Charter Arms snub-nose model. Called an 'Off Duty.' There's the serial number. Write that down for me, Cox, will ya? It's K1015618."

"Got it."

Rasco draws the gun to his nose. "This gun's been fired recently. Smell that Jeff; I think we've got our weapon. It's fairly well oiled; prints might be hard to come by, I'm afraid, but we'll see. What about the sweatshirt? See any blood?"

The team knows that collecting dry blood by applying moisture is standard procedure. But leaving it moist could damage or even destroy whatever evidence that might come from the sample.

"Nope. Color's too dark. You'll have to send it to the lab. Just in case it does have blood, you could let it dry. We can always moisten it later. May have to freeze it. What's that?" They all saw something drop from the pocket.

"Appears to be a small piece of a latex glove, I'd say, with a dark smudge on it. Might be blood. Potential evidence." Everyone agrees with Rasco, whose specialty is homicide investigation. "Let's take a better look at the weapon. Four fired casings. One left in the chamber."

"Same number of shots the girl says she heard." Millslagle

rubs his chin as his eyebrows knit closer together. He glances at Rasco. "But what's the weapon doing in the girl's closet?"

"Good question. Look at this t-shirt. Looks like blood spatter on the front to me. This kid loves the name brands. Tommy Hilfiger."

Rasco still studies the gun. "There are wear marks here as though something was mounted on it. Doesn't look that new either."

Millslagle stands up as his foot nudges something underneath some dark sweatpants. The object is black and metallic. "Laser sight for a firearm. That's what you're looking for, Joe. It'll probably fit that barrel."

"Evidently." The laser sight fits perfectly on the snub-nosed .38. "Ya know, I just can't see this little girl knowing how to attach a laser to a gun. It doesn't make sense."

Rasco places the gun in a plastic bag, staples, and labels it.

Millslagle notices that the middle drawer is pulled out of the daughter's chest of drawers, and the sliding doors of her closet are off their tracks. He moves toward the bed. A gold-colored gift bag on a shelf above the bed catches his eye; he examines it. Pink-colored tissue paper is stuffed inside along with a hundred dollar bill. "Nice gift."

Detective Cox lets out a guttural humming sound. "Look at this. A damn hole cut in the back wall of the closet along the edge of the flooring." He sticks his hand in but finds nothing.

"I'd say this is recent work."

Rasco continues to take pictures, including the hole.

"The girl says she heard footsteps in the hallway and in her room." Cox, Millslagle, and Rasco conduct several tests throughout the residence, including walking from the master bedroom area through the kitchen, living room, down the short hall, and into the bedroom of Stephanie Barron. Cox, who is of medium weight, meanders through the areas in various ways, from light steps to heavy. Neither Rasco nor Millslagle, who crouches inside the closet, can hear Cox until he arrives at the doorway to the bedroom.

"That's interesting." Rasco makes several notes.

The room is unremarkable other than the gun, laser attachment, stained clothes, and gift bag, which Millslagle takes special interest in. As in any normal bedroom, framed photos cluster together on top of the chest of drawers—photos of the daughter's friends, which include several black males giving obvious gang symbols. The men recognize most of the boys in the photos. "Not a good sign," Millslagle says through a sigh.

This is the first step in crime investigation. And the most critical in terms of evidence gathering. All law-enforcement agencies have unsolved crimes, and the team knows full well that murder is the crime most likely to remain unsolved because the victims do not survive to tell their tales. So far in this case, no witnesses saw the killings, which complicates the investigation. The difficulty of solving homicides of this type is why there is no statute of limitation for the crime of murder.

Rasco the artist often likens the initial stages of detective work to the under-painting of a work of art—a layer of paint that hides beneath the final image in a finished piece of art. The under-painting sets the direction for the art yet is buried beneath the final colors and details of the painting. It is the crime-scene investigation team's job to begin with the under-painting of a crime scene. The clues are there, sometimes beneath the surface. It could be shades of gray or thin, quick washes of color. This is where the process begins. For an artist, it is called inspiration and an eye for design; for a detective, it is intuition with an eye for detail.

Rasco looks around. "Anybody from the DA's office here yet?"

"No, but I think that's the sheriff's car pulling up."

Everyone knows when the sheriff arrives. He does not have to be the first one at a crime scene because that is not his job. But he often shows up at some point. They turn toward the sound of the sheriff's boots in the short hallway. Rasco is a little surprised he is here today.

"Good morning, Sheriff."

"Good morning, my ass. It's cold and it's Christmas. Are you tellin' me we got a damn double homicide on Christmas? Aw, shit. Ain't there nothing sacred anymore?"

"Yeah, seems there's always something happening on a big holiday."

"Hello, Millslagle. This the daughter's room?"

"Yes."

"Well, well, well." The sheriff notices on the left edge of the closet doorway that the daughter apparently wrote, "I love Dinario," using the heart symbol. "Could be a boyfriend. He's most likely in one of these photos. You'll need them, Rasco."

"The word *denarii* means silver or gold coins from third century BC Italy. It originally meant the equivalent of ten asses. If you spell it with an *i*, *dinari*, then it refers to paper or coins in the Middle East, Iraq, Jordan, Kuwait." Rasco remembers this from his travels in that part of the world while in the Air Force.

"You're a smart ole ass, Rasco. It's probably a nickname. Hell, with names these days, you never know."

"Maybe it means 'I love money.'"

# CHAPTER SIX

## Chili and Commode Wine

Not just any beer-drinkin', backyard-grillin' guy can cook competition chili. I got nothin' against beer drinking because for some people, eating chili's not the same without a beer. October is the month I often judge the International Chili Cook-Off in Teralingua, Texas. I am a connoisseur of Texas chili, and I know the protocol that competition chili demands. The first rule about chili is no beans. Nada. No way. It's all about the meat and gravy. You put beans in your chili, and I'll throw your sweet ass in jail. Not without a proper warrant, of course. Now remember, I'm talking about competition chili. You earn points along the way. Competition chili is judged on five levels: color, aroma, consistency, taste, and after-bite.

The color can't be too light or too red. The aroma is either there or it's not, and an expert knows the aroma when he smells it. The consistency of the gravy can be too thin, and the beef cubes can be too thick. You've got to get that strong chili taste; it can't be too sweet or too hot, and the cubes must melt in your mouth. And finally, the after-bite has to tell you that levels one through four have been perfect. Then you change spoons, cleanse the old palate with a beer, and move on to judge the next pot of chili. I tend to burp a lot, but I don't think chili people mind because there isn't anything wrong with burping when you're as serious as I am about judging. Hell, it's good for the digestion.

The procedure for cooking and judging chili is like any kind of step-by-step protocol, even in law enforcement. For example, I remember the steps we went through after answering a call from dispatch during my days as a California cop and Tyler patrolman. The first officer to arrive on the scene must take certain steps to preserve his or her life and the life of a possible victim. That's exactly what Sergeant Hendrix did at the Barron murder scene. The next thing is to protect possible evidence by cordoning off the area as soon as it's safe and secure. Then Hendrix called for assistance.

Analysis of the crime scene begins after the personal safety of everyone is assured, and that's when Rasco, Cox, and Millslagle went to work. Could be that someone needs medical help. Hendrix determined the need of emergency medical services. Depending on the level of danger, the officer might need backup firepower or firefighters.

Then there's the problem of figuring out who might be witnesses or suspects and separating everyone so they can't agree on their stories. Finally, the first officer establishes a security log for anyone who enters the crime scene. Like judging chili, protocol can be complicated and requires a high level of training and experience, but that's what it takes.

I noticed as soon as the reports started coming in that the Barron murders seemed to be calculated and certainly cold-blooded. Hell, it doesn't take a forensic scientist to see that. In the Barron case, the perpetrator obviously shot the victims at close range, a few feet from the corner of the bed on Mrs. Barron's side. The DPS crime lab in Austin confirmed that it was not murder-suicide and concluded that the swabs we took from the Barrons' hands did not have any gunshot residue—antimony, barium, or lead. That was consistent with what Rasco thought at the crime scene.

An odd thing happened that Christmas morning: Stephanie Barron ran away from the detectives and into the bathroom during the initial interview. She locked the door. Detective Cox said it sounded like she was throwing up, but he noted that she might have been washing her hands. At the time, she was not a suspect, just a little girl who had lost her parents.

Crime scene and follow-up investigations in the lab are critical. Lab work has evolved into quite an accurate and sophisticated science with trace-metal residue tests for firearms, fingerprinting, and DNA. Depending on the type and condition of the weapon, we may use neutron activation analysis on a suspect's hands where gunpowder residue might be. Usually the more efficient the weapon, the less gunpowder it will produce. On the other hand, an older, inefficient weapon with a misaligned barrel and cylinder will produce lots of gunpowder. Maybe even a very small slice off the bullet. We also use chemical sprays that reveal under a black light whether or not a suspect has held a gun recently. Sometimes we can tell how a person held the gun, which is especially important in a possible suicide.

Fingerprints at the Barron murder scene were negligible. Fingerprinting is a damn art form if you ask me. Those guys know their stuff, all about arches, loops, and whorls. Most prints are loops. Fingerprinters can even take an ear print. We were hoping to get prints from the latex gloves we found at the Barron house because in some cases we have lifted prints from thin gloves, but we didn't find anything. December is not the best time to gather prints because they just don't last as long as in the summer. The heat and humidity of the East Texas summers make it somewhat easier. Don't ask me why 'cause that ain't my job; that's just the way it is. So we had a little disadvantage due to the time of year. Latent prints are ones that you don't see readily—usually not until the item or area is carefully dusted or sprayed, which is part of the art. The timing is usually about a ten to twelve hour window for lifting prints.

Many people know from watching television that it's possible to find clues from hair, from minute material underneath a fingernail, and of course, from blood, saliva, and semen. All these clues can tell stories and lead to exposing the perp, but I can assure you it's not as easy as it looks on TV. The level of a juror's sophistication is going to get higher due to television, and that could put more pressure on the prosecution because juries will expect more proof. They think our job is quick and easy.

DNA information is fascinating, although more time consuming. People accused of crimes have been convicted and cleared on the basis of DNA. It reminds me of taking a slice of a tree and studying the rings to tell the history of the tree and how it survived wet or dry weather and fires.

The autopsy report performed the day after Christmas at Mother Frances Hospital Morgue indicated that Carla Barron took a shot to the left side of her face near the nose—front to back and slightly upward, which could show that the perpetrator was not exceptionally tall. The bullet lodged in the back of the skull. The killer apparently was not an accurate shooter because, although it was dark, the second bullet hit the victim in the arm. We got that bullet too.

In the Barron case, we learned a lot from the lab work. Since there was no evidence of a struggle during the murder, we didn't have a lot to work with except the murder weapon, ballistics, and the daughter's clothes. So we had to look further. It turned out that Stephanie Barron ran with a group we were familiar with.

John Tyler High School student Dinario Jones was likely a gang member. He always carried a gun, and he stole for money to buy and resell drugs here in my county. The lure of all that likely had a lot to do with his relationship with Stephanie Barron, although he was probably not the first black male she dated.

Gang-related crime has been going on here in Smith County for years. Many young people join gangs to be a member of a family, in large part because they're not getting a sense of belonging elsewhere. Gangs think they're above and beyond the law and operate according to their own rules of reward and punishment. But I'm the law here in Smith County, and if I catch anyone, gang member or not, I'll stuff their butts in jail.

Incarceration has become the main arm of social control rather than the home, the church, or the community. And it's damned expensive to house all these perps in Smith County. I know. I'm the one who comes up with the budget. And we're running out of room, so I have to send my prisoners to jails in other counties, which is more expensive than keeping them here. I've said it many times: we need a new jail, but nobody seems to pay attention.

I know jails because I run one of the biggest county jails in Texas. I'm the "Boss Man," as the inmates call me. So I know how it works. Occasionally I'll talk with an inmate and he'll promise me I'll never see him again if he can just get out. Most return. So as I see it, the system has it backwards. All that money the government spends on adult rehabilitation should be put into the highest-quality, day-care facilities. Maybe these centers can target problem children. Because by the time these problem kids reach junior high school, it's too late. Maybe the behavior of these two seventeen-year-olds could have been spotted earlier, and perhaps intervention could have helped. The Barrons tried to intervene. All along, Dr. French thought that Stephanie Barron had the predisposition for a psychopathic personality disorder. Those types don't care how their behavior affects others. They're stuck. They're in a dangerous rut, and as I always say, the only difference between a rut and a grave is six feet.

The impressionable Stephanie Barron bought drugs, drank alcohol, and skipped school after she mixed with the wrong crowd. As far as gangs go, it's pretty easy to see they don't bond like normal people. It's the wrong kind of bond based on violent acts by members of the group. Many young criminals are very egocentric because they don't think they can get caught. They fantasize on what it would be like to kill someone and often get high and randomly pick somebody to kill or rape. It's their initiation into the group. That's why we call them gang bangers. They respond to gang mentality.

Since Stephanie remained the prime suspect, Dr. French

thought that something in her mind might have triggered her to kill her parents because of her association with Jones and his friends. Let's face it. To kill your parents, you gotta be pretty damn cold-blooded, and that, to me, is a psychopath.

Wade French tells me the emotional level of a psychopath has no depth. They don't understand love or compassion for others. They can't internalize guilt. Their sex lives are driven by lust and thrill. The fear of consequences for their antisocial or criminal behavior has no long-term effect on changing their behavior because they don't consider getting caught. They have a limited ability to learn from experience. By adolescence, most normal youths have developed a conscience primarily driven by the very emotions that don't develop in psychopaths. For psychopaths, their behavior is focused on two concerns. First, identifying victims to satisfy their needs regardless of how this affects the victim, and second, avoiding detection. So here we have the life cycle of the psychopath, and almost all behavior can be explained and understood from these two driving motivations. They learn early and easily the role of a predator.

Psychopaths can be arrogant. Many criminals brag about their exploits. Matter of fact, that's when a lucky break in a case comes: the perpetrator says something about a prior crime to a cell mate when he's in jail on another charge, and we find out. Sometimes we hear their communication when they dip the water out of the commodes and talk through the plumbing. They don't realize we can hear them when they yell down the toilet. Now we have automatic flushers because the inmates figured out how to make wine by keeping their fruit and mixing granulated sugar to the water in the commode. In seven days they could make alcohol. "Commode wine" we called it. Prisoners say it can get you fallin' down drunk, but it has one hell of a tangy taste, I'm told. I believe it gives true meaning to one of my favorite sayings, "This tastes like shit."

The year 1999 was a strange one. Maybe it was because of Y2K. In addition to the Barron murders, there was another tragic incident that year. A fire occurred in October. It provided critical ballistics evidence relating to the murder weapon, which proved our case in the Barron murders.

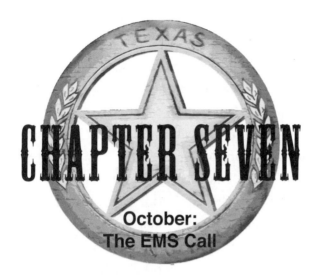

# CHAPTER SEVEN

## October:
## The EMS Call

In the early morning of October 25, 1999, Shelley Rae Haynes can barely breathe. She calls 911 and requests help as she speaks from the floor of her bedroom. Nearly unconscious, the young mother manages to say her house is burning while gulping scant oxygen below the level of thick smoke.

**1:56 a.m.**

Dispatcher McDonald at Tyler PD calls EMS headquarters. Operator Wesley Hicks quickly relays the information to the nearest ambulance staging post.

The dimly lit communications control center is quiet. The large room is darkened so the men and women on their twelve-hour shift can operate under optimum visual conditions. They talk softly. Time compliance allots thirty seconds for an operator to gather the address, call-back number, and nature of the problem from a caller. The next thirty seconds are for the operator/controller to contact the closest ambulance. That is the protocol.

Operator Hicks sits in front of three monitors and occasionally looks up at the south wall where an enormous screen continuously shows Doppler radar for an area between Dallas and Shreveport. On the left is a smaller monitor displaying the Weather Channel. On the other side of the radar screen, another monitor reveals the various surveillance shots from cameras positioned inside and outside EMS headquarters. The time is visible on a large atomic clock below the radar screen and is perfectly synchronized with all emergency agencies.

Hicks receives the call. He immediately goes to his radio, an eight hundred-channel trunking system that automatically picks the first available channel to contact a staging post. He keys up, relays the information to the nearest ambulance, and carefully places two critical terms in his brief message: "Priority A," which means lights and sirens, and the word "trapped." That one word means someone is inside a burning residence and cannot escape.

A few miles away, eighteen-year-old Lauren Kirk watches a Western movie on television. Blankets and pillows are piled in one corner left of the TV. The room, full of day-old, take-out cartons of fast food and cups of flat soda, is in a motel at the intersection of Highway 69 and Loop 323. Another person, a young male, smokes outside the room. Lauren has been here many times. It is the north-side emergency medical services staging post.

The ambulance, or "truck" as they call it, is parked outside the door. The truck houses a row of cabinets on either side full of meds, portable trauma kits, and equipment for stabilizing patients while in transport. A gurney or spine board sits to the left, which leaves just enough room to go from the back doors to the front. A bench seat on the right extends almost the full length to the captain's chair, which faces the rear.

### 1:58 a.m.

"Priority A at 833 Blackwell Street. House fire, two people trapped." EMS operator Hicks's voice breaks the drone of the television.

Lauren, a graduate of EMT basic, is an intermediate, an EMS worker-in-training and enrolled in EMS classes at Tyler Junior College. She is being trained in all pre-hospital trauma care, including evaluating and stabilizing trauma patients, rapid assessment, aggressive resuscitation, packaging, and transport, but she cannot perform advanced paramedic patient care yet.

As in evaluating a crime scene and dispatching emergency services, EMS specialists follow their own protocol. Lauren's job is to help with basic resuscitation techniques and to drive an ambulance. Throwing on their gear, she and Scotty, her supervisor, rush to the truck and roar off through the large intersection. It is a short trip to Fifth Street.

### 2:06:30 a.m.

From Fifth Street, Scotty steers the truck left onto Palmer Street and travels past the parking lots and soccer fields. A quick right and they arrive at Blackwell Street where two houses blaze with intense heat. Several firemen try desperately to quash the flames, but the corner house is consumed. The house next door is going fast.

"This fire's been going for a while."

"Yeah. Wonder why we just got the call."

Scotty's first response is to size up the scene before he and Lauren approach the patients, as victims are called before assessment. All Scotty knows is that there are at least two people who may or may not be trapped inside the house by this time.

The obvious dangers at this scene are fire, electricity, and smoke. The patients may need to be removed immediately. Scotty and Lauren carry two long backboards from the ambulance. Lauren checks the straps, head immobilization devices, and spinal collars. Scotty grabs two trauma boxes, which include bandages, blood pressure cuffs, stethoscopes, and two oxygen airway kits.

Firefighters have valiantly removed two individuals from

one house. They are unconscious in the backyard. Scotty decides this is not a generalized, high-energy event that would include injuries such as those from a gunshot wound. This is called a focused event, which includes possible life-threatening injuries from smoke, fire, or a fall.

The patients might have head or neck injuries, so Scotty and Lauren approach the patients from the front. They will not need to turn their heads if they regain consciousness. Scotty yells, "Pedi!"

Lauren runs back to the truck for the pediatric trauma box and smaller backboard. This is the only trip back they have time for. The pedi kit contains everything in a smaller size including a bulb syringe for clearing nasal passageways.

Children come first. Scotty kneels by the little girl with short, curly, blond hair that is about the color of Lauren's. He tries to resuscitate the child while Lauren attends to the adult female. Neither trauma victim responds. They might be suffering from hypoxia, head trauma, shock, seizure, or smoke inhalation.

Scotty's rapid trauma assessment takes less than two minutes. Lauren readies the smaller backboard, quickly arranges the C-collar and airway equipment, and expertly stabilizes the little girl's neck by carefully placing a small blanket beneath her back and shoulders. As Lauren turns back to the adult, she places the trauma box next to the backboard and sees that the female's head is at an angle. Not wanting to rotate the neck, she gently immobilizes the head by placing a folded blanket under the right side of the face and taping the area for stability. They prepare both victims for transport. Their goal is to return to the ambulance within five minutes of arrival.

### 2:09 a.m.

Around the corner from the fire, Sheriff's Deputy Robert Britton steps out of his home and sees a young male standing beside a gray and maroon Dodge pickup parked in the yard nearby. The young man slowly rides his bicycle down the hill to watch the fires.

The noise and excitement draws a small crowd of neighbors. Lauren looks up and sees two young men watching intently, one on a bicycle. She glances at the child, still motionless on the gurney. The little girl is wearing white Mickey Mouse pajamas.

Fortunately, no one is home at the house on the corner, 829. But the power has not been cut to the second house, and the electrical lines rain fire. Soot, ashes, and now sparks from above pelt the two EMS workers, compromising their situation and making it too dangerous to continue.

"Load and go!" Scotty yells to Lauren and the second crew. EMS workers carry the mother and daughter to separate trucks and take them away.

Scotty drives. Lauren pushes the oxygen bag with a two-handed squeeze, then compresses the anesthetic bag while holding back tears. She forces her mind to focus on the job at hand—the child's breathing—because mask leaks can cause 40 percent loss of critical oxygen. She turns the face mask upside down for a better seal on the child's face.

In a clear voice with slow delivery, Scotty radios the hospital emergency room to prepare for their arrival, relating the urgency of the situation.

"This is EMS Unit 210 calling ETMC ER."

"This is ER nurse Nancy Evans. Go ahead Unit 210."

"Unit 210. Paramedics leaving the scene of a house fire with one pedi, age three or four, female, and one adult female, mid-twenties. Possible smoke inhalation. Patients are unconscious. Weak palpable pulse but no sustained breathing. Giving oxygen and CPR. ETA about five minutes. Requesting an IV to maintain blood pressure. Base, how do you advise?"

"IV will be ready. Transport ASAP."

"Copy. Returning to dispatch frequency. Unit 210 clear."

In their cramped quarters, a fireman methodically presses the girl's chest. Finally, as they near East Texas Medical Center Hospital, the fireman stops pressing. Lauren looks up, stunned, and sees the man lay his hands on the little girl's chest.

"Dear God, please put life back into this child."

Lauren has never seen anything like this before. Part of the job is to be somewhat detached, to perform the duties she has been trained for. But she is paralyzed. This is not exactly textbook procedure. She stares into the face of the fireman, then drops her eyes to the little girl. The child starts breathing. Lauren becomes hysterical and unable to continue as they reach the emergency entrance of the hospital.

**2:14 a.m.**

Her name is Hannah. As they prepare her for a flight to Children's Medical Hospital in Dallas, Lauren picks leaves from the child's hair, smoothing it back away from her face. Attendants rush Hannah to an idling helicopter waiting on its pad—an island in the middle of the parking lot adjacent to the hospital. The helicopter will take Hannah to Pounds Field and to a waiting EMS Air One jet. After silently telling the child good-bye, Lauren glances to her left; nurses rush Hannah's mother to a hyperbaric chamber for emergency oxygen treatment.

They are losing Shelley. She is taken to a monoplace pressure chamber to breathe 100 percent oxygen at a rate two times the normal pressure. Shelley will receive up to fifteen times as much oxygen to her tissues as she would normally receive breathing room air. The increase in pressure is equivalent to what a scuba diver would experience from twenty-two to thirty feet below the surface of the water.

EMS physicians have not recorded any brain activity. Shelley looks like a little sleeping doll in a plastic pneumatic tube, the kind customers use when they send a deposit to a drive-through bank teller. The acrylic, cylindrical chamber is eight feet long and three feet in diameter. The immediate goal is to increase blood vessel diameter, improving blood flow to Shelley's compromised organs.

### 3:10 a.m.

Scotty finds a spare chair in the hallway and fills out the paperwork: run call number, scene description, age, sex, injury, and time. He notes appearance, vital signs, and level of consciousness from his primary survey at the scene. Considered a legal document, this report will be kept with the patient's records.

When he finishes, they drive slowly to breakfast at the IHOP on the south Loop. Scotty, Lauren, and a friend from the second ambulance enter and sit across from the kitchen in the back where they can smoke. There are a few customers who look like students. The kitchen is not very noisy.

Scotty and Lauren smell like smoke as they read the menu. An older man who sits by himself notices. He asks if they had a rough night, and Scotty replies softly, "Yeah, but we'd rather not talk about it."

### 5:00 a.m.

Shelley Haynes never regains consciousness.

### Noon

Hannah dies in Dallas the following day.

# CHAPTER EIGHT

### John Sneed

'm a sheriff, not a clinical practitioner like Wade French. But I do study the criminal mind as it relates to unnatural behavior. And I'm curious. One of the peculiar things about the Christmas Day homicides was where the murder weapon came from. It was stolen from the house in Tyler that was intentionally set on fire to cover a burglary, although officials originally determined the cause as a faulty electrical outlet behind the television set. And frankly, there wasn't anything to make officials think otherwise at the time.

When firemen arrived inside the Haynes home, they heard the smoke detector, but it wasn't mounted on the wall. It sat on a small, waist-high table in the hallway. If the detector had been higher, Shelley and Hannah might have had more time to escape. We know their house had been burning for some time, maybe as long as an hour according to fire department officials. But Shelley and Hannah didn't realize it in time. We think Hannah heard the alarm and went to her mother's bedroom to wake her, but it was too late. We'll never know for sure.

A fascination with fire is not exactly normal if you ask me. I love a winter fire in my fireplace, but pyromania is pathological fire setting. Dr. French tells me it's a compulsive disorder and a symptom of anti-social behavior. Could be a frustrated sexual drive. Hell, I've read reports of perverts who watch the fires they set and become sexually aroused to the point of orgasm. Now that's sick.

Here's my point. By stealing a gun from the house on Blackwell Street, the arsonist implicated himself in the Barron murders. Events surrounding the fire and murder led Detective Rasco to Beth Little, the owner of the burned house and stolen gun.

Beth Little's father, a pastor in Conroe, Texas, told us he bought the gun at the Oshman's sporting goods store in Houston. Protection for his daughter was important. He went to the trouble to build a wooden storage box with green felt lining and a small, Styrofoam area for bullets. He gave the box to her, along with the .38, about ten years prior to the Barron murders. He said he bought an identical replacement at the Oshman's following the burglary. Mr. Little thought his daughter needed it for her own safety. He was right. She needed it. And she kept it loaded.

The myth of "honor among thieves" is exactly that. A myth. It just ain't true. Those of us in law enforcement operate in a selfish world—a world where the criminal element acts like a damn pack of sharks that feeds off itself. One will turn against another if there's any gain to be had. A cold call is one that's unsolicited and unexpected. A person in trouble comes forward with information that might help his case or harm another's. They will turn in their own mothers before they will take blame for anything. It's never their fault. Sometimes the claims defy logic, but we get lucky, and the claim turns out to be immensely helpful. In January 2000, Major Lusk, chief of CID, contacted Joe Rasco with information from one of those calls.

"I just got a message from a guy who wants to talk to the detective that's working the Barron case. He didn't leave his name or anything."

"Where is he?"

"Corner of Highway 110 and the north Loop, an Exxon station. He wants you to pick him up so he can talk to you about the Barron case."

"You think it's legit? I mean, do you know anything else?"

"Nope. Just wants to talk."

"OK. What's he driving?"

"Didn't say. I think he's a black guy from the way he talked. He'll be standing by the phone booth or a gas pump there at the Exxon waiting for you."

Rasco and Detective Jim Gholston went to the Exxon station. For a meeting like this, no detective wants to go alone because too many bad things can happen.

Gholston drove around the gas station parking lot three times as they searched for a young black male. Rasco spotted a white youth standing by one of the pumps. He was wearing the typical, butt-cracking, baggy pants and an oversized, long sports jersey.

Rasco asked him, "Hey man, are you the one who called us about some information?"

"Yeah, I waiting for the detective on the Barron case. He the one I wan' talk to."

"I'm Detective Rasco. What's your name?"

"John Sneed."

Rasco easily saw why Major Lusk made the mistake of thinking the young man was black. He talked and dressed like a typical gang banger. He wore a jersey-type, pullover shirt with a large "p" on the front.

Without asking any questions, Rasco and Gholston took Sneed downtown for questioning. During the ride, Sneed volunteered that he knew Stephanie Barron, who had been at his girlfriend's house the day before the murder. Rasco was very interested, but said nothing.

Sneed had been sent to lockup in August of 1998. He and his mom got into a violent argument, and he went to my jail.

76

John Sneed

Sneed told Rasco he had information and wanted to trade for some assistance with his legal problems. Rasco did the right thing—no deals.

"Well, you have to understand we can't promise you anything," Rasco hedged. "I will tell the DA in that county what you have done for us, but I can't guarantee it will help you. Do you have an attorney?"

"No, sir."

"Do you want an attorney?"

"No, sir. I done need no attorney."

"I'm listening."

Sneed was a skinny kid with short-cropped hair. My generation called it a burr cut.

As they continued toward downtown, Sneed started talking again.

"Detective Rasco, do you 'member a fire in the city dat killed a woman and her little girl, her baby?"

"Yes, that was on Blackwell Street, I believe, in late October. I remember reading about that in the paper. Since it was inside the city limits, the Tyler Fire Department handled it because that was all there was to it. Accidental death. Terrible."

"Yeah, well the laws says it was accident, but I know who set dat house on fire."

"It was deliberately set?" The information made Rasco want to believe him, even though he knew from experience that most informants are habitual liars.

On videotape, John Sneed related that, although he did not know much about the Barron murder, he did know about the house fire.

Rasco said, "So what can you tell us about the fire?"

"Which one? The car fire or house fire?"

"Let's start with the car fire." Rasco didn't let on that he had not been aware of a car fire until Sneed mentioned it.

"Well, Dinario tol' me he stole Stephanie's car and burn it to make it look like a burglary. That was why he burn it."

"Did you see the car before it was found?"

"No, but Dinario drive us pass the area, you know, where it was, but we didn't actually see it."

"Where was that?"

"A place call Devil Hills off back behind Trane in south Tyler."

General Electric had opened a plant in 1956, and Trane bought it in 1982. The company manufactures residential central air-conditioning units.

"Did he take anything from the car before he burned it?"

"Yeah. Stereo player, CDs, speakers. I think there was a speaker or amp in the trunk. He cut his finger he say and got blood on the car. Maybe dat was another reason he burn it."

"Did he mention a gun in the car?"

"A gun? No. But dat would not surprise me."

"Why is that?"

"He carry a 9 mm with a wood-like handle at all times. If

78

parents were not around, he'd take it out and put it nearby, but he usually carry it in his waistband."

In a follow-up interview, an acquaintance of Sneed's stated it was not Jones but Sneed who burned Stephanie's car. The acquaintance said Sneed's girlfriend told him that, John Sneed, another friend, and she did it because John wanted the stereo deck. The acquaintance said Sneed threatened him and promised revenge if he said anything.

Rasco asked John about the house fire.

"I know who dun it. It was set deliberate to cover a burglary, like the car. And it was Dinario Jones. Stephanie told me he did it."

"How long have you known Dinario Jones?"

"I've known him a while—maybe a year. We all hang, me and Dinario, Stephanie, and Ashley, my girlfriend. He broke in dat house 'cause nobody was home and stole a television set, some jewelry, and a gun. He hid the stuff in bushes. Yeah, it was him all right. Stephanie say he panicked after he stole the stuff and went back and burned the house to cover the evidence of his burglary. He was worryin' 'bout fingerprints, you know."

"Do you know if Dinario Jones has been involved in anything like this before?"

"No, not really. I mean he steal stuff 'round here and sell it in Dallas, but man, people got kilt in dat fire."

"How did he feel about that?"

"He didn't say, and I couldn't tell. He done talk much."

"Anything else you want to say to us?"

"Well, I do know he ride his bicycle down to see the fire. The woman was on vacation, so that's why he rob her. But dat fire went next door, you know."

Rasco continued prodding Sneed for more information. "Is there anything else about Stephanie Barron? Did she ever mention killing her parents to you or in front of you?"

"Yeah."

"How often?"

"It was probly four or five times she say she wan' to kill her parents."

"Did she say how she would do it?"

"Mainly she talk 'bout shootin' 'em. She once say she might put a bunch of scorpions in der bed. Dat way there wouldn't be no blood."

"Did you ever see her shoot a gun?"

"Yeah."

"Was she a good shot?"

"No, she was turble. She couldn't hit nothin'. That's probly why she bought that scope thing."

"You mean a laser light attachment?"

"Yeah, yeah, that."

"How did you know about the laser?"

"My girlfriend tol' me."

"Did she talk to you about the murders?"

"All she say was she shot her dad furse. Then her mom wake up and look right at her. And she shot her. Twice."

"She shot her dad first. Why do you think she did that?"

"Well, I got my ideas. He probly had a gun close by. The other thing was 'cause she was disgusted with physical abuse by her dad. She told Dinario dat, and he tol' me."

"What kind of physical abuse?"

"Her dad would hit her, you know, I mean he would knock the livin' shit outta her."

"Why?"

"He did not like Dinario 'cause he black. Her dad would yell at her and call her a ho and slut for dating a black guy. Hell, the black thing had nuthin' to do with it fo' Stephanie. Anyway, I done think he was the furse black person Stephanie dated. She also say her dad punch her pretty bad after she run away a few months ago."

"Did Dinario talk to you about the murders?"

"Yeah some. He did say Steph call him the night of the murders and want him to help her do it dat night. Dinario say he would help, but not to do it right now. He wan' wait and plan it so it would look like a burglar broke in and shot them, you know. But she would not wait. Das where she got the idea of someone breaking in. She call him again from her grandparents' house after she shot her parents. Dinario tol' me that, but he wouldn't talk to her."

"Anything else? Did Stephanie say anything else about her

parents?"

"Only dat they did not seem to show much emotion. Her mother was always axin' Stephanie to go to church with her, but she would not go."

"Did either one of them mention money to you?"

"Yeah, Stephanie was 'posed to get 'bout $500,000 from her parents."

"Where was that coming from?"

"I done know 'cept it was in their will or somethin' like dat."

After getting new info out of this Sneed character, Rasco terminated the interview and called Tyler PD to explain the information. He also called the fire chief to ask if by chance anyone had videotaped the small crowd of onlookers at the Blackwell Street arson. Often the arsonist is at the scene, as Jones had been, according to Sneed. Unfortunately, no dice; there was no videotape.

"So now this is a homicide case you got," Rasco said to Detective Clay Perrett at Tyler PD.

"That's what it looks like, Joe, if this kid Sneed is telling the truth."

"I really think he is."

"So Jones burned the house, and he burned Stephanie Barron's car that was reported stolen from her home."

"Yes."

It was another case of blind luck for us. So the investigation moved forward with the new information about the fires and stolen gun and would bring to light the relationship between Dinario Jones and Stephanie Barron. Ballistics on the stolen weapon would reveal the final pieces of this puzzle.

# PART II
# THE INVESTIGATION

# CHAPTER NINE

## Friends of Stephen Barron

O K, Detective, give me the latest on the who, what, where, why, and how."

"Yes, sir. You were at the scene, so you know the who: Stephen and Carla Barron.

"It's front-page stuff, photos and all. It's damned amazing."

"As far as the perpetrators, I'm not sure of the 'who' yet, but the only suspects I have are the daughter and her boyfriend. She was there at the time, but I'm not certain about the boy. We haven't found any evidence that clearly puts him at the scene, but I think we will. The 'what' is obvious—capital murder—and we're putting together a motive, but that's going to take more time. The 'when' is one of the remarkable things about this whole crime. Of course, you know it was Christmas Day."

"Right. Nearly froze my butt off." J. B. leans back in his leather, wing-backed swivel chair with the state of Texas insignia behind his head. The chair is not that comfortable, but he loves the color and the insignia. His office is in the southwest corner of the fifth floor. In that corner is an L-shaped bookshelf with photos of United States Senator Kay Bailey Hutchinson, President Reagan, and the Bushes, various gifts and memorabilia, including a knife from the Himalayas from a writer friend at *The Dallas Morning News*, a set of *Vernon's Texas Civil Statutes*, and a large volume of *Criminal Law and Its Processes*, all behind the sheriff. To his left is a gun rack handmade by his stepfather. It holds two commemorative Winchester Model 94 rifles. On the other side of the desk sits a hand-crafted saddle made by one of his deputies and mounted on a stand. The sheriff's name and title are chiseled on it. Detective Rasco sits in one of two leather chairs directly in front of J. B.'s desk.

"'Where' is obvious. The Barrons were murdered in the bedroom of their trailer. Did you see the two dogs in the bed with the victims? They were still and quiet the entire time we were at the scene. I wonder what happened to those dogs."

"Any problem with trace evidence? It's easy to get fiber, human, and dog hair mixed up, you know."

"Right, Sheriff. Lots of variation in form and structure when it comes to unattached hairs. Of course, when you have two dogs living in the house, you're gonna have lots of hair. There are obvious differences between human and animal hair. These dogs were short-haired, so I don't see any problems. I hope someone's taking care of them."

"What about 'how'?"

"How is going to be easy, I hope, because we're prepping what we consider the murder weapon for tests. Remember the gun we found? We get a match on bullets, and we've got a case. Items of clothing with blood, too. They're already in the crime lab. Autopsies took place the day after the murders. I'll be interviewing two of Stephen Barron's friends later today."

J. B.'s eyes twinkle as he grins at Rasco. "Detective, you're right on top of things, right where I expected you to be."

Rasco nods as his eyes break contact with the sheriff's. He looks at something on the sheriff's desk he's seen and admired many times. It is a custom oak box with display glass. Inside is a 125-year-old Sheriff's Model Colt .45, probably owned by Dan Tittle from the Oklahoma Indian Territory. Tittle's name, place, and date of death (1901) are inscribed inside the grips. The modified Peacekeeper six-shooter was a gift presented to the sheriff in August 1999. The modifications, probably done in 1884, include a shorter barrel and the elimination of the ejector rod and housing to accommodate the newer .32-20 caliber. This makes it easier to conceal and easier to draw. Perfect for a sheriff back in the old days when the law was the gun: "shoot first and ask questions later," as the saying goes.

J. B. notices Rasco eyeing the weapon. "Yep, the three

notches on the grip obviously mean something. Dan Tittle was well known in those parts for being a very bad hombre."

People in law enforcement become familiar with guns and bad characters. They are part of their life. Everyone has their favorite gun. Smith County peace officers buy their own on-duty weapons, but many own more, everything from shotguns to Derringer-type pistols small enough to carry in a Western boot. The agency confiscates hundreds of weapons each year. The way they are disposed of is set by law.

"This Tittle fella. Was he originally from Texas?"

"Don't know for sure, Rasco, but it wouldn't surprise me. Rasco, you know it's a damned shame when tragedy strikes this time of year as it's done in the Barron family."

"Right."

"From all accounts, Stephen and Carla Barron led normal lives for the eighteen years they were married. 'Course, they never celebrated Christmas, you know, due to her religion."

"And Mr. Barron worked hard in the construction business in Dallas. Mrs. Barron seemed to be a typical housewife and mother. But she increasingly had trouble disciplining her daughter. Maybe that's typical, too."

"Have you interviewed any of Stephen Barron's friends?"

"Yes, sir. About two years before the murders, Mr. Barron began a dialogue with a longtime friend about Stephanie's behavior, her friends, and her promiscuity. One thing that greatly concerned the father was that he worked out of town.

90

So he wasn't able to consistently discipline Stephanie. Barron told his buddy he was having problems. Said his daughter was writing hot checks. He was also pretty upset about her choice of friends, especially boyfriends. Barron's friend wrote in a sworn statement to me that Barron told him that Stephanie was a follower. You know, easily influenced by others. At the father's insistence, his daughter finally changed friends."

"That didn't seem to help the situation. What about Mr. Barron's boss?"

"Mr. Barron's supervisor at Commercial Finishing Company in Dallas stated that he last spoke to Barron on the Thursday prior to Christmas."

"Was he happy at his work?"

"Don't know. I can talk to his employer again. It turned out her new friends were worse than the old ones. That's what Barron told his buddy. And accordingly, the daughter's attitude changed for the worse, too."

"Tell me more about Mr. Barron's friend."

"Evidently he was with Stephen Barron the night of the murders. He had known him for over thirty years. Helped him burn leaves that Christmas Eve. That evening Mr. Barron told his friend that he grounded Stephanie for not closing her overdrawn checking account as he ordered her to do. According to the interview, Stephanie told her mother that she had no intention of closing her account. This kind of conflict caused by the daughter drove Stephen Barron to consider leaving the marriage. He confided in his friend that he couldn't take much more."

"Please don't tell me that the daughter might have killed her parents because they grounded her. God almighty. You know, Rasco, I wouldn't try to raise kids these days for nothing. Too much going on. Too many bad things out there."

"Right, Sheriff. But we haven't proven she did it, you know. I've gotten a conflicting report from the mother of Stephanie Barron's friend. She said in a written statement that Stephanie was a good kid who always did what her parents asked. And, as far as the mother knew, she had a good relationship with her parents."

"Smells like bullshit to me."

"Could be. At any rate, we are dealing with a young woman who shows two sides of herself. Depending on the situation."

"Sounds psychopathic."

"Could be. Another longtime friend of Mr. Barron's stated that according to Stephen, his daughter was irresponsible. She refused to follow the rules of the house. Often threatened her mother with the idea of running off when she didn't get her way."

"Sounds kinda manipulative, if you ask me."

"In written testimony, this other friend stated that Stephen wished Stephanie were eighteen. Then she could move out because of the conflicts she caused within the family and because of the arguments with her mother. I get the definite impression that the father seemed discouraged. I think he was fed up with Stephanie's attitude and mistreatment of her mother. Especially since the mother's surgery. The conflicts seem to parallel Stephanie's association with a rough crowd of students at Chapel Hill High School."

"Peer pressure. Any more information about the murder weapon?"

"Not from the lab. By the way, Mr. Barron's first friend I told you about said that he had recently seen Stephanie practicing with a .45 handgun in her backyard. She appeared to be a pretty good shot, considering she had not been around handguns that much. I'll bet practicing with a weapon is likely due to her gang friendships. As far as her school activities, the counselor has no documentation of any counseling sessions with Stephanie. No discipline problems. The principal and the campus police say the same. No problems. I've got interviews with Stephanie and Dinario scheduled."

"Sounds like to me that many times Mr. Barron returned home from Dallas to discipline his daughter because his wife could not or would not. Hell, this kind of thing can split a man in two: a troublesome daughter who required his attention and a job a hundred miles from home."

## CHAPTER TEN

### Friends of Carla Barron

**T**he day after Christmas the sheriff and his team started lining up people so they could make some sense out of the Barron murder case. A critical part of the process is interviewing acquaintances of the deceased and other people of interest. One of Mrs. Barron's close friends arrives on the fifth floor of the sheriff's offices for her interview with Detective Joe Rasco.

#### 9:00 a.m.

Dixie Whitbred sits easily in one of the two metal chairs next to a filing cabinet opposite Rasco. He guesses she is about forty-five years old, attractive, well dressed, and probably 5'5" and in good shape. She wears a blue jacket, jogging pants, and running shoes.

"Ma'am, you said you talked to Stephanie Barron the day of the murders. What did she tell you?"

"Yes, I went over to their house as soon as I heard about it. Stephanie didn't say much. I think she was in shock, honestly. Stephanie said she hid in her closet after she heard some gunshots. Had her phone but her line was cut. She didn't know why they only cut her line. She ran out down the hall after she saw a shadow and got scared. She didn't appear very nervous, probably in shock, like I said."

"You were good friends with the deceased wife, Carla Barron, correct?"

"Oh, yes. Carla and I were very close and spoke quite often about lots of things. Carla had been worried that Stephanie was hanging around with the wrong kind of kids for the last couple of years. She was rebellious, like lots of them. Carla told me that Stephanie went with a friend and the friend's parents on a vacation and the girls stole the parents' car and left. To come back I guess to be with their friends. At least that's what Carla thought."

Rasco leans back in his squeaky chair and strokes his chin with two forefingers.

"Does Stephanie have a boyfriend?"

"Yes. And that was part of the problem. Stephanie lied about being with the boy. Probably because of her daddy. Carla saw the boyfriend driving Stephanie's car one day with her at his side. They spent a lot of time together, according to Carla. Carla told me that about one and a half years ago, Stephanie ran away. I don't recall why. But she was grounded for sneaking out of her bedroom window. Two boys picked her up. Probably the boyfriend. Gone about a week, I'd say. Stephanie got very angry at her father for grounding her. My husband and I were at Steve and Carla's often, and they told us how scared and worried they were about Stephanie. Carla started crying when Steve said how concerned they were that she might get pregnant."

"Can you tell me anything else about the boyfriend?"

"Not much, really. I do recall that Stephanie was arrested for forgery of a check. I asked why she did it. Carla said Stephanie told her she wanted to give her boyfriend a birthday present. So she gave him the money."

"How did Mr. Barron feel about that?"

"Steve didn't like it, for sure. I know Carla didn't trust the boy a bit, although from what she said she never got to know him that well. Steve told me and my husband he didn't like them dating. He told Stephanie that, too."

"What was Stephanie's reaction when her father said that?"

"Oh, she got mad again. Not in front of her dad, of course. But she was mad, all right. Stephanie always seemed to take everything out on Carla."

Rasco pauses and checks the clock while he sips black coffee. On either side of the clock hang the only two photos in the office: a skyline of Seattle where his daughter lives and a mountain scene with a stream cutting through a wooded area. Rasco enjoys realistic photos and art, although some impressionistic paintings are very interesting because they're similar to a crime investigation. Sometimes a person gets too close to a painting and loses sight of the composition. When an investigator gets too close to the facts of a case, he cannot step back and see the whole picture. Objectivity is critical.

"Mrs. Whitbred, what kind of parents were the Barrons?"

"Well, pretty normal I'd say. They were strict. Especially Steve. Jehovah's Witnesses, you know, although it was basically Carla's religion. Stephanie wouldn't have any part of it. I thought Carla tried to be a little overprotective at times because of Stephen's temper. Stephanie took advantage of that, I think. Many were the times when Carla and I talked on the phone. And Stephanie would yell at her mother to get off the phone. Finally she would. I do want to say that I've never heard a bad word about the Barrons. Not one word."

"Tell me more about Stephanie Barron. What about school? Friends?"

"Here's something I'll never understand: Stephanie was an A/B honor roll student at Chapel Hill. But she dropped out of school, supposedly to help Carla recuperate from her brain surgery. I would ask Carla about Stephanie helping her out. Carla would say that Stephanie usually stayed in her room and talked on the phone. Carla suffered from headaches and sometimes had trouble walking with her cane. Would Stephanie help? No, not according to what Carla said and what I saw myself. But she never acted disrespectful when my husband was with me or especially when her daddy was home. It was just with Carla. She threatened her mama about moving out and getting her own truck and apartment. But her father insisted she wait until she turned eighteen and got her GED before he would allow her to move out. She tried to go back to school. Didn't work out. Don't know why. Honestly, after a while I think Stephen was ready for her to move out."

"So they were having family problems?"

"Yes, sir. Carla told me many times that she thought Stephanie was lying to her about all kinds of things. They were burglarized once. Carla wondered if Stephanie and that boyfriend had something to do with it. So they had an alarm installed after that. Another time she was driving the truck and came back without her dad's toolbox. She said it slid out of the truck when she took off too fast. By the time she turned around to get it, someone took it. Well, that just didn't sound right to me. She could have sold it or traded it for drugs."

**10:00 a.m.**

Rasco sits with his back to two large windows that frame the opposite block between Erwin and Elm Streets as another of Carla Barron's friends is escorted in for interviewing. The old Tyler Theater, long since closed, is in need of restoration, but it probably won't happen in Joe's lifetime. Now a blight on an otherwise attractive downtown area, it was at one time the center of teenage social activity. Guys would "sit" with a girl. "Sitting" could lead to a date to the dance. Kids ate cold dill pickles, popcorn, and Baby Ruths. Nobody watched the movie.

Rasco looks down on the street below, the large antique store beneath the Fair Foundation Building and the Lindsey Building, each full of oil-leasing agents in the good old days. Those who grew up here remember the moving neon arrows that pointed the way to the Tyler Theater's entrance from the corner of Erwin. With a sigh, Rasco turns back toward Mrs. Henney.

"Ma'am, how well did you know Carla Barron?"

"I met Carla about six and a half years ago at a little pharmacy on East Fifth Street. It's closer to Chapel Hill. It's that little gray one-story with the blue trim a little ways from the Loop going east. I filled her prescriptions. We got pretty close two years ago because of health problems we both had."

"Did you know the daughter?"

"Not at first. Carla always spoke of Stephanie in a good way. But last year Carla had a brain tumor removed. That's when Stephanie started giving Carla problems. You'd think it'd be the other way around—that the daughter would help her mother. But no."

"What kind of problems?"

100

"Fights. After Carla came home from the hospital, Mr. Barron wanted Stephanie to stay with her. You know, drop out of school and take care of her mother. But Stephanie didn't like that. She only thought of herself and her friends. Stephanie got into a fight with Carla, and Carla said Stephanie pushed her. And Carla just home from the hospital. That's when Carla told me things were not going good."

"Yes, ma'am. Anything else that you know of?"

"Well, Stephanie ran away after that. Carla was very upset, of course. She finally found her at some boy's house. They saw her and drove off, but Carla thought they were still in the house. She must have stayed there for a couple hours, then Stephanie called her mom's cell phone and asked if she could come home. So she did. A boy showed up. Same one, I guess. He tried to explain a few things to Carla, but she wouldn't talk to him."

"How did you find this out?"

"Carla, she told me this over the phone that night. We talked about it, and Carla felt like she was losing her daughter."

"Did you ever talk to the daughter?"

"Yes, once. When Carla used the drive-through at the store one day, I saw Stephanie through that window on the west side of the building and told her about things I did when I was her age. You know, trying to be her friend and maybe help Carla. She told me to mind my own business. I know it embarrassed Carla to no end. I felt really sorry for Carla. She didn't deserve this kind of thing."

"Did Mrs. Barron ever mention drugs in connection with her daughter?"

"Yes, sir. A few nights later Stephanie's friends showed up at her window and gave her a Coke. It must have had something in it. You know, like a drug. Because Stephanie told her mother she passed out and when she came to, she couldn't remember a thing. She was at some motel. Said she'd been raped all night. Worked over pretty good, sounded like to me."

"Did Mrs. Barron call the police? Were charges filed?"

"No, not that I know of. Stephanie called her mom, and Carla went to get her. Carla came to the pharmacy and told me about that. At least that's the story she got from Stephanie. I wondered about it though."

"I see. Is that all you know about any drugs?"

"Yes, sir."

"Any other problems you know of?"

"Well, some time in October, maybe early November, Stephanie had a car accident. I rode with her to the ER. Stephanie was very agitated because she did not want her mother upset. I thought that was kinda nice for a change. She seemed all right until her mother and Mrs. Toner showed up. That's the grandmother. Then Stephanie switched back to her attitude. She seemed to have two sides, you know. Sometimes nice and sometimes with an attitude. I guess that's normal for kids that age. Things seemed to get better after that."

"What happened?"

"Well, Carla and I talked at the store and on the phone quite a bit. We were close. Things were getting better, I think, because Stephanie finally quit school."

"To help her mother recover, right?"

"Yes, sir. The story I got was she dropped out because she was scared of some kids at the high school. So she got her GED. She's a smart kid. Honor society and all. The last day I talked to Carla was five days before Christmas, before she died. She said things were great between her and Stephanie, and they were getting closer. I believed her. I could tell she was happier because she loved Stephanie and wanted the best for her. Maybe being away from those kids at school helped. I don't know. Then it happened. It's just terrible. The Barrons were nice people. They didn't deserve to die that young. I feel a real sense of loss. Like any friend would, I guess. I hope to God the girl didn't have anything to do with it."

Although Stephanie Barron has consistently denied any involvement in the shooting death of her parents, Detective Rasco sees some inconsistencies in her story. He needs more physical evidence to make a charge of capital murder stick. He has what everyone considers the murder weapon. The leuchomalachite green field test for blood on one of the stains indicated a strong positive reaction for blood on the girl's shirt. The matching pants were taken to the crime lab for testing because of the dark color. That could help too. The latex gloves found in the kitchen near a plate of cheese balls might be significant. Gloves in the back of Mr. Barron's truck and the partial ones in the daughter's bedroom could add to the case. Nothing remarkable was found on the clothes in the washer-dryer in the laundry room.

Detectives utilized metal detectors to look for any additional fired bullet fragments in the lawn area just outside the window and where the bullet's path was indicated by the trajectory from the master bedroom. Nothing there, except an old fired .22 casing.

It's the bullets fired from the gun. If the fired bullets match the weapon found in the daughter's bedroom, and if the weapon can be tied to Stephanie Barron, we might have the case solved. *But there seems to be something missing*, Rasco surmises.

He recalls Stephanie stating that she did not actually see anyone or hear anyone talking and did not hear a vehicle leave the scene. Someone could have parked on the county road about twenty yards from the house.

Rasco looks at the ceiling. *Come to think of it*, he muses, *she didn't say she heard the dogs either. But if her boyfriend is involved, the dogs may be familiar enough with him. Another thing. She's small. So I suppose she could hide in that little closet. It's a tight fit.*

As usual, he keeps an open, but suspicious, mind.

**2:00 p.m.**

"You were a friend of the deceased, Mrs. Carla Barron?"

Evie Abbott is tall and slender. She has the look of a school librarian with her horn-rimmed glasses that rest halfway down her nose. She is dressed in a black suit with a white blouse buttoned all the way to the top. Ruffles ripple down the front. She has the East Texas nasal twang Rasco has grown accustomed to. At least she speaks distinctly.

"Yes. Good friends."

"Tell me about your relationship with Mrs. Barron."

Ms. Abbott peers over her glasses. "I got to know her quite well. We talked a lot. Carla was a very caring, sensitive person. Maybe too sensitive. She told me she was afraid for Stephanie because she was running with a wild crowd at school. That was her word—*wild*. And she took advantage of her mother's illness by skipping school. That was my opinion, anyway. Carla was afraid Stephanie was using drugs supplied by her boyfriend. Stephen put an alarm in the house to keep the boyfriend out and Stephanie in. It didn't work."

Rasco leans back in his chair. There had to be more of a connection with the boyfriend who sold drugs. Rasco looks at Mrs. Barron's friend and asks, "Why didn't it work?"

"The alarm? Well, she somehow got boys in her bedroom. Everybody thought Stephanie was pregnant by the boyfriend. I suppose it could have happened anywhere, not just in her bedroom. Carla said she thinks Stephanie often let boys in through her window. I think she could have gotten pregnant by any number of young men. That's what Carla said. She also told me Stephanie got pregnant once already and had an abortion in Dallas. The way she was acting was just killing her parents."

"Did her parents confront her?"

"Yes, I heard about it when Stephen found out about the hot checks."

"Do you remember any other incidents of the daughter's behavior? Anything about early childhood? Excessive punishment by her parents?"

Rasco has seen many cases where kids get off track when they grow up in abusive situations. Sometimes that pushes them to join gangs.

"The only thing would be her friends. Carla said Stephanie needed money often. I never knew of any stealing except from her parents. But you know kids. They're all about themselves, deceitful and immature to a point. Stephanie was defiant and rebellious. I know that Stephanie stole things from her mother. You know, money and coupons. She wrote those hot checks and got in big trouble. I suppose that's stealing too. I think that might have been a turning point with her dad."

"How's that?"

"Well, Steve was the authority. He's the one who set the rules. That hot-check thing really set him off, and he let

Stephanie know about it."

"Did you ever see them yelling at each other?"

"No, sir."

"Anything else?"

"Yes. I helped Carla find Stephanie after she went on a vacation with a friend and her family. The two daughters stole the family car and took off. That was a while back. Poor Carla was dying inside. I know she was. Recently, Stephen gave Stephanie a final ultimatum, as he called it. He told her to close her checking account and stop seeing the boyfriend. She needed to straighten up or he would kick her out, not pay for her legal bills, and take her out of their wills and off their insurance. That happened the day before Christmas Eve, as I recall."

# CHAPTER ELEVEN

## Stephanie Barron and Dinario Jones Interviews

**R**asco notices that Stephanie Barron is a pretty calm and cool little girl. Hard to believe she is really seventeen years old. She looks straight ahead and never wavers from what Rasco considers a vacant stare. Maybe she is in shock. Stephanie seems to be an odd mixture of emotional maturity within a childlike physical appearance.

On the second floor, Stephanie Barron waits in a lobby with Officer Bobby Garmon. Rasco continues on to the sixth floor and into the secured area where CID detectives work. Rasco has found no records of problems at school, nothing to indicate a history of antisocial behavior. A student has come forward to say Barron has been getting into fights with other girls lately, but the student has not been interviewed. Although diagnosis is not Rasco's job, it helps to develop a psychological profile of suspects to get a handle on possible motives, to build a solid case, and to put the bad guys in the pen. Rasco likes to say, "You do the crime, you do the time." He got that line from the sheriff.

### December 25, 4:00 p.m.

"Come with me." Officer Bobby Garmon escorts Ms. Barron to interview room number one where she meets with Detective Rasco. She is dressed in jeans and a yellow, over-sized football jersey, somehow inappropriate for the occasion. She is neither intimidated nor hostile.

"Ms. Barron, you've been Mirandized, so you know you can have lawyers present. You haven't been charged with anything."

"Yes, sir. I'll talk to you, but I didn't do anything."

"You should also know you are a critical witness to the events that occurred early this morning. It's important that you tell me everything you can remember. Again, anything you say can and will be used against you. Understand?"

"Yes, sir."

"Tell me what happened."

"I already did that. I wrote it all down." She throws him a pouty look.

Rasco sternly glances away. He allows her to think for a few moments. "Yes ma'am, I know, but we need to go through this again."

"Well, I heard four gunshots that woke me up. I hid in my closet and closed the doors and tried to call 911, but my phone wouldn't work. I heard someone in my room, and he was going through all my drawers and took a hundred-dollar bill. When I thought he left, I slid open the closet door and ran as fast as I could to my grandmother's house. She didn't answer the door, so I banged on the bedroom window. Granny called 911 to report a robbery. And I talked to a lady, too, the dispatcher. That's about it, I guess."

"Did you say you heard three gunshots?"

"No, sir, it was four. Definitely four."

"And you say you hid in the small closet in your bedroom?"

"Yes, sir, that's what I already said."

Again Rasco pauses. "Why didn't you exit through the front door? It was only a few feet from your bedroom. You ran the entire length of the house to get out."

"I done know. The back door was wide open. I guess I was scared. We done use the other door much."

She slips. Rasco easily recognizes some gang-type slang. The contracted word *don't* is replaced by *done* and rhymes with *phone*. The smart ones understand code switching, using the appropriate language for the appropriate occasion. Teens speak one language at home or with friends, another in the classroom unless a teacher tolerates slang. Rasco is a traditionalist when it comes to Standard American English.

"Your boyfriend. He's black, right?"

"Yeah, so?"

"Did your parents have a problem with you dating a black person?"

"Oh, I done know. Maybe. My mom's not crazy about it. But my dad's not a racist or anything. We broke up, me and D. I pissed him off. But we still might get married some day. That would be after I get out of college and he gets out of the military."

The daughter speaks of her parents in present tense, as if they were still alive.

"Who is D?"

"Dinario Jones."

*Revenge against her parents for not approving of her boyfriend sounds like a possible motive,* Rasco thinks. But there is more. The gang-banger boyfriend has something to do with it. That is one of the first things law enforcement tries to do: establish motive, means, and opportunity. Maybe it was that simple, after all. Maybe her parents' strict discipline from a religious and military point of view motivated her. The insurance money, the house, the vehicles would produce money for drug buys if her parents were dead. If she committed the crime, she might not have realized that the insurance company would not pay on the claim if she was convicted of killing the insureds. She probably never thought about that. Just a kid. Kids never plan on getting caught.

"Ms. Barron, have you ever used drugs?"

"No, sir."

"Would you say you have fairly normal relations with females and males your age?"

"Yes, sir, I do."

Rasco does not respond to Ms. Barron's answers, but he notices something. Her body language starts to send messages. She leans forward and makes contact with her green eyes. She stares at Rasco while he speaks. It is as though she is interviewing him, which would probably unnerve a rookie. For her age, she is very persuasive. She is trying to take the offensive. Rasco wonders how the child of a stable family can be questioned in a sheriff's interview room about the murder of her parents and remain so calm.

"Ms. Barron, tell me about your friends."

"I got lots of friends. We do fun stuff, you know, normal stuff like teenagers do. Sometimes girlfriends come over and spend all weekend."

"You never got into trouble, you and your friends?"

"No, sir. We just hang out and talk."

"Where?"

"At our houses. Sometimes the mall."

"Spend any time at Dinario Jones's house?"

"No, he doesn't want us over there. We meet about a block away. I pick him up."

"Why is that?"

"I dunno. Something about his mother."

"Ms. Barron, what was your father like?"

"I love my parents. Dad gets mad sometimes, and he's strict, but I love him. Me and a friend and my parents, we all went to eat at Red Acker's Restaurant last weekend and had a real good time."

"So you got along pretty well with your parents?"

"Yeah, sure. We have lots of good times. You know, family dinners and all. Their friends come over. Yeah, it's pretty normal."

"Did you ever fight with your parents, physically? You said your father got mad. Did he ever strike you?"

"Oh, no, nothing like that. Dad's got a temper, but like I said, we're pretty normal. He used to be in the military, but that was a long time ago."

Barron continues to speak of her parents as if they were at home, waiting for her to return from her job at the donut shop.

"Being in the military, do you think that's why he was strict?"

"Maybe. I dunno. I don't see him that much."

"Anything else about your father you want to tell me?"

"Dad helped me pick out my car. He let me choose the color. I love my car. I'm really lucky to have one; not everyone has a car like mine."

"And your mom? Did you two get along?"

"Absolutely. She helps me a lot with my homework and stuff like that. I took care of her because she had this tumor in her brain. They got it out though. I'm really thankful for that."

"I believe your mother went to church more than you and your father. Did they ever pressure you to go to church?"

"Well, not exactly. I really didn't understand her church, the Jehovah's Witnesses. I know they don't believe in eternal punishment or the Trinity thing. Something about being able to know God and understand him. My mom says that's impossible, to understand God like that. My friends think it's pretty weird, but I really don't talk about it. I can't have blood transfusions either. They don't believe in passin' blood around 'cause of diseases."

Rasco wants to pick up the pace. "Ms. Barron, what about this hot-check charge? How did your parents feel about that?"

Stephanie squirms just enough for Rasco to notice. "Well, they weren't exactly cool about it. It's my account and my money. I got it taken care of. But I got grounded again."

"And the forgery?"

"I needed some money for D's birthday present. That was all. I just didn't have any money at the time. Mom and Dad were pretty mad about that. Besides, we done celebrate birthdays 'cause of her church. But I can celebrate with D if I want to."

"Ms. Barron, what did you do the day before the

murders?"

"Well, I got off work from the donut shop about 12:30."

"How long have you been working there?"

"'Bout three weeks. Then I went to the bank at the Brook-shire's on Rice Road and cashed my paycheck for $327. I got home about 1:30. Mom was there. I gave her $160 for car payment, insurance, and attorney's fees for the forgery."

"Where was your father?"

"At work, as usual. Even on Christmas Eve day. You'd think he'd come home, but we done do Christmas anyhow 'cause of Mother's church, so it done matter. Then I went to Longino's Bail Bond to check in 'cause I'm sorta out on bond, you know, for the forgery. Then I went to the mall, then home."

"Were you with your boyfriend all this time?"

"No, sir. By myself. When I got home, my dad was there with mom. We didn't say much. I told them I loved them and hugged Dad. I gave him my car keys. That's the rules. I've been grounded 'cause of bad checks and the forgery, you know. I can only drive to work and to my cousin's house. They let me drive to the school for my GED."

"What about the night of the murders?" Rasco abruptly changes the subject in an attempt to throw her off guard. "What did you do that night?"

"I went to my room to watch TV. A little later, my mom said she had friends coming over to have a bonfire out back and watch a movie. Man, a bonfire and a movie on TV. That done sound like fun to me, so I took a nap. When I got up, I saw out the window that part of the yard was black. My mom came in, and I asked her what happened. She said that Daddy caught the grass on fire. She also said that their friends were not coming over because they had too much to do 'cause of Christmas and all, I guess. So it was just one guy that came over. Mom went back outside, and I went to my room. She finally brought the turkey in the house and cut it up. I ate some in my room while watching the movie *Piranha*. They were watching the same movie and eating in the living room."

According to Stephanie, the Jones boy did not make an appearance the night of the murders, but Rasco thinks he is a part of all this. He cannot let go of it. Jones and Barron have been seeing each other for a while. He may have used her for sex and for her car so he could buy drugs. In turn he and his friends protected her, a familiar gang-style relationship.

"What did you do after the movie?"

"I fell asleep. Around 10:30, I woke up and turned the lights and TV off. Then I woke up again when I heard the shots and heard someone walking around my bedroom, like I already said."

"Stephanie, you said you didn't see anyone, but you did see a shadow. I personally conducted tests in your house. I was in your bedroom while another detective walked all over the house. I couldn't hear him, and my hearing is pretty good."

"That's what I heard!" Her thick lips turn pouty again. Her

voice grows more urgent. "Someone was there and stole my money!" She looks toward the door and slowly says through closed teeth, "I've already told you that."

She makes quick hand movements now as she pauses between sentences, then makes larger gestures while she speaks. Rasco thinks she may be struggling to keep her composure. He presses her.

"Stephanie, you said you closed the closet door while hiding from the gunman. But the sliding doors were off their tracks, which would make that impossible."

"Well I done remember that." She slowly rubs her hands together.

It is Rasco's turn to lean forward and stare. He lowers his voice. "Usually people who wake up in the middle of the night don't always remember the exact number of gunshots. But that's what you said: four gunshots. Not some gunshots. Four."

Stephanie is silent.

That is exactly what Rasco looks for in an interview or investigation, something that does not quite fit. First the sliding closet doors off their tracks, now the specific number of gunshots, the shadow, the footsteps. Detective Rasco tries to keep an open mind, but it is getting harder.

**December 26, 1:45 p.m.**
FBI Special Agent Jeff Millslagle leaves FBI headquarters

118

in the third floor of the BancAmerica building located inside Loop 323. Driving north toward downtown Tyler, he travels the short distance to Fifth Street near Tyler Junior College. Turning on Palmer Street, Agent Millslagle arrives at Dinario Jones's residence northeast of the junior college. Jones lives with his mother. The house is a one-story, red-brick structure in an average neighborhood, one that was once a nicer place.

Millslagle confronts Jones through a screened door. Jones is wearing only shorts.

"We want to talk to you about your whereabouts last night."

"I was with friends."

"Where was that?"

"At apartments in south Tyler, near the Braum's."

"How long were you there?"

"'Bout two hours, maybe three. Then my friends took me home. I talked to a girlfriend 'til around midnight, then went to sleep."

"Mr. Jones, I'm taking you downtown for more questioning."

Jones's mother is now behind him. "Don't you arrest him! You can take him, but don't you arrest him!"

"Ma'am, your son is not under arrest. We just want to talk to him."

Jones says nothing during the ride to the sheriff's head-quarters where Detective Rasco waits. Jones is a very streetwise kid. He does not talk. He sits motionless while looking out the window. He wears a smug look well.

"I'm Detective Joe Rasco. State your full name."

"Dinario Therrell Jones."

"Mr. Jones, you knew the Barrons and their daughter, Stephanie, so you know why you're here."

"That's right. I know Stephanie, but we're not a couple, you know. We're not dating or nothin'."

"But you were dating each other at one time."

"Yes, that's true."

"What was your relationship with her parents, the Barrons?"

"I had no relationship with the Barrons. I didn't know them. I was never there."

"What about the daughter?"

"Well, I met Stephanie Barron awhile back and started dating her around Halloween this year. But I done know nothin' 'bout no murders."

"What about your relationship with the Barrons?"

"Like I said, I had no relationship. But Steph's mother did hassle me 'bout me being the reason Steph wrote them hot checks. So I broke up with her by phone and have not spoke with her by phone or in person and have not paged her since then. Except she call me at home yesterday."

"I thought you never talked with the mother, but you just said she was hassling you."

"Well, yeah, but that was through Steph. Steph would tell me stuff her mother said 'bout me."

"What did she say when she called you?"

"She say something bad happened, and I told her I done care and hung up on her."

"And you don't know anything about the murders?"

"That's correct. I done know nothin'."

"Do you own a weapon, Mr. Jones?"

"I do not."

"Do you know how her parents felt about their daughter dating a black person?"

"Yeah, I know. Stephanie tol' me her parents done like black folks and done want her datin' me. Thas OK. I done like whites. But we didn't break up 'cause of that."

Rasco asks again, "How long did you date the daughter?"

"Not that long, really. Over a year. I broke up with her two or three weeks ago 'cause I found out she was fuckin' another guy."

"What's his name?"

"I done 'member."

"But you know the guy?"

"Yeah, I seen him around."

"Have you ever been to the parents' home?"

"I have not. I have never been to Stephanie's house. We always met at a friend's house. Sometime she would meet me near my house."

"So you don't know why anyone would murder the Barrons?"

"Like I said, I never knew them. Maybe Stephanie knows."

"Do you know anything about Ms. Barron's car that was stolen and burned?"

"Not really. She let me drive it. I had a set of keys."

"So you never talked to her parents? You were never at Stephanie's house, and you two have broken up?"

"Thas correct. Well, actually, her mother did call me once. She said that Stephanie and I had to break up 'cause it was all my fault. Stephanie been arrested for a bad check and was in jail. When Stephanie got out of jail on bond that same night, she call me. It was then that I told her I knew about the fucking, like I said, and I broke up with her."

"And you haven't talked to her since then?"

"I have not seen or talk to her since then, except for her call yesterday morning 'bout somethin' bad happened."

# CHAPTER TWELVE

## Born to Be Bad

**W**hen I was a boy, my escape was the movies. I loved Westerns starring Roy Rogers, Gene Autry, Hopalong Cassidy, Lash LaRue, and Johnny Mac Brown. Movies cost ten cents at the Pastime Theater in Warren, Arkansas. It was all so clear cut then. The good guys, wearing white hats, rode on Palomino horses with fancy saddles and always rescued the pretty girl. They beat the bad guys with black hats and dark-colored horses with plain saddles. These B-rated movies played an important part in my life and the way I thought life ought to be. Now I've got a beautiful horse with a fancy saddle.

Since this morning's big glass of fresh-squeezed orange juice, without the vodka, I've been thinking about Stephanie Barron and her possible mind-set on Christmas morning.

Maybe the violence in video games, cartoons, and movies contributed to her psychotic state of mind. Wade French tells me a normal person sees about 2 percent of violence in a movie. Another person with schizophrenia recognizes five times that amount. If you combine a psychiatric disorder with substance abuse, then the individual sees as much as ten times the violent episodes in the same movie. When it comes to watching violence, it's all about perception based on our backgrounds and lifestyles.

Two movies come to mind, *Natural Born Killers* and *Piranha*. You'll see some extraordinary psychopathic killing in *Natural Born Killers*. In that movie, Mickey and Mallory murdered around fifty people before they went to prison. That's probably a record for anything except a war movie. Later in the film, Mickey and Mallory killed more people than I could keep up with during the prison riot. About halfway through the movie, Mickey was the only calm person, much like a psychopath. He was, in a very bizarre turnaround, circumspect amid all the chaos. He conned everyone. Another interesting psychopathic trait was Mickey's hold on women. They loved him; he had them in his power. The so-called psychiatrist in the movie stated that Mickey was not insane because "he knows the difference between right and wrong. He just doesn't give a damn."

In her jail cell prior to the prison break, Mallory sang about "born to be bad," a sure sign of a psychopath. This movie should be required viewing for those interested in psychopathic traits.

The important trigger for his psychopathic killing spree was meeting Mallory and finding a kindred spirit. She hated her parents, which made me wonder about Stephanie's relationship with her parents and with her kindred spirit, Dinario Jones.

Stephanie Barron watched *Piranha* on Christmas Eve. *Piranha* offered plenty of violence, but there were two significant incidents that could have affected Stephanie. Here's my take on *Piranha*. It's bad. I'm not a movie critic, but as people say about whiskey and women: I know what I like. The unquestionable image depicted by the main character in *Piranha* was clearly of a psychopathic predator. He killed without conscience because he made his own rules.

Two siblings, a brother and sister, arranged for a photo trip into the jungle with a guide. About two-thirds through the movie, I noted a reference to family murder. As a little girl, the daughter watched their mother blow their father's brains out after many years of quarrelling. Stephanie's anger and intolerance with her father's insistence on rules might parallel the mother's feelings in the movie too. Stephanie saw other violent images of rape and murder in the movie. Finally, the sister of the dead brother, who was murdered by the predator, found his rifle and killed him. I don't want to get too analytical, but Stephanie Barron might have identified with the predator's mind-set of wanton killing and his own rebellious sense of authority.

Thumbs down.

Violence in movies, on TV, and in video games can have a detrimental influence on young people. But the one thing that comes back to me is that some kids are born to be bad. They enjoy being evil.

I'm sitting here on my back porch thinking about the idea of nature versus nurture. It most likely takes some of both to shape a person, but I've seen some definite factors that shape adult behavior, such as genes, the cycle of poverty, and child abuse. Peer pressure, too, like Stephanie Barron's friends put on her.

Stephen and Carla Barron tried to create a healthy environment for their daughter. Stephanie Barron could very well have had some kind of psychotic genetic tendency. Dr. French would call it a predilection toward psychosis, such as paranoia that revealed itself when her environment changed during her socialization with a rough bunch at school.

Often at a critical moment in a teenager's life, the influence of the parents and the security of the home are replaced by the influence of friends and activities that go on outside the home. This is part of their environment. It's obvious that Stephanie Barron yielded to the mind-set and lifestyles of her friends rather than follow the wishes of her parents.

I've heard this about people all my life: "He's just like his papa." I think some behavior is shaped from generations of the same lifestyle, mind-set, and gene pool. Nobody's got the balls to say that these days because it's not politically correct. But you know, as I grow older, I've become more cynical because I've been around so many damn perverts and perpetrators.

In Appalachia, people are geographically and socially isolated, poverty stricken, and somewhat inbred. I'm not talking about stereotypes; I'm talking about facts. It ain't no big deal to marry the girl next door, even if she's your first cousin and has the same last name. Reminds me of some of those characters in the Burt Reynolds movie, *Deliverance*. Matter of fact, only recently has it become illegal in Texas to marry your first cousin.

I was born to an unwed mother in Sumptor, Arkansas, in a house without electricity. That's deep in the back country. To get to the main road into town, we rode in a mule-driven wagon on a dirt path that was so rough we nearly bounced out of the wagon. If we didn't hold on tight to something, we could be thrown out into the dense wilderness and never be seen again. At least that's what my mama warned us about. I held on as tight as I could.

I came from poverty. We had plenty of food; we just didn't have much variety. All we had to eat growing up was beans, cornbread, and pork. All meals had some kind of pork because we raised hogs. Big suckers. My granddaddy would shoot one in the head, then we would scald it in a fifty-gallon barrel of boiling water. As the oldest boy I had to sit astride the hog and scrape the hair off the hide. This happened every fall, and Lordy I dreaded it more than everlasting fire and damnation. God, it stunk. It was the same as going to hell and coming back. So I wasn't malnourished, but many people were then and still are, and childhood undernourishment can affect brain development. That's what French says. My point is that an environment that can make a person miserable and even dangerous doesn't always produce long-term consequences.

Other events can affect brain development. Everybody in my business knows that Arthur Shawcross, who murdered eleven prostitutes, suffered from brain damage from blows to his head, which probably produced a cyst on his brain. This is the guy who cannibalized parts of his victims. He was so screwed up, he had multiple personality disorder. I think it resulted from child abuse and brain damage.

The complicated issue of how to judge violent criminals always comes down to this: are they mentally ill or evil? My view is that if a person knows the difference between right and wrong and commits a violent act, he's going to jail. If a criminal is sick, he needs help, but he's not going to get much in prison.

Based on his experience, Wade French is convinced Stephanie Barron needed help because of her psychopathic behavior. Others may disagree, and that's fine. But I tend to go along with French. Psychopaths are experts at manipulating other people, especially the opposite sex. One woman married Ted Bundy after he was convicted of murdering at least thirty women. He was a damn predator, and he wormed his way into women's lives. I've heard stories of prison psychologists, who should know better, falling in love, having affairs, and marrying inmates they're supposed to be counseling. As I recall, a prison nurse recently killed a guard because the man she married, an inmate convicted of armed robbery, told her to do it.

Just this year, a convicted robber went back to prison after another attempted robbery ended up in a shoot-out with the police. He married a woman while in prison the first time, and after his release, they had two children. She helped him write a best-selling novel about his life. He's got plenty of time to write now, back in prison.

Even highly educated women succumb to predators who show incredible skill at taking advantage of a vulnerable situation. A predator can spot a weaker human being and exploit that person to get what he wants. Now, I'm not saying women are the weaker sex because my wife would whip my ass for saying such a thing, but I am flatly stating that a psychopath will take advantage of a situation, whether that person is male or female. He doesn't care about hurting anyone as long as he gets what he wants.

In the Barron murder case, Dr. French believes that Stephanie preyed on the weaknesses of her mother. Carla

Barron loved her daughter and probably tried everything she could think of to keep peace in the family, from what I can tell. But Stephanie took advantage of her mother's sympathy, according to testimony of family friends.

The human predator, like animal predators, is impulse-driven in his self-created world of survival. He or she, by the way about 2 percent of imprisoned psychopaths are female, will commit any crime as long as it brings them pleasure, because guilt doesn't play a part in the equation. Some criminals slow down around age forty and blend into society, but not psychopaths. They're dangerous until the day they die. I call them bad to the bone.

# CHAPTER THIRTEEN

## January:
## All's Fair in Love and War

Although Stephanie Barron planned to marry Dinario, he apparently didn't agree. One reason was because he couldn't keep his pants zipped. I don't think Stephanie ever accepted the fact that he couldn't be faithful in their relationship. Hell, she wasn't exactly a paragon of virtue either. But I think she might really have loved him. Some people are like that. Then we discovered a student at Robert E. Lee High School who said she was Jones's new girlfriend. We don't know how long this relationship was going on, but Stephanie found out. According to a source at Lee High, the Lee girlfriend said that Stephanie called her the day before Christmas Eve and told her she would kill her if she didn't leave Dinario alone. The student found the message on her home phone and deleted it. She didn't want her mother to find out. The student also said that Jones had not helped Stephanie Barron kill her parents because he had been at her house until around midnight. He left after a loud argument they had on the front steps. Hell, that would still give him plenty of time to get to the Barron home, since the shootings occurred around 4:00 a.m.

The Lee student further stated that she found out a car had been stolen and burned and that it belonged to Stephanie Barron. Jones torched the car because he had clothing and other personal items in there that he didn't want us to find. We'll never know what the items were unless he tells us, and you can forget about that, but whatever he destroyed might have connected him to the murders. Our source said to the girlfriend that Jones could very well go to prison for stealing and burning a vehicle, and the student shrugged her shoulders and said, "Yeah, I know that." Now that's true love.

In this business, you never know where your next piece of information will come from. A female from Henderson County entered the Smith County low-risk jail. Because of medical problems with her pregnancy, we had to move her to the downtown facility, A-tank. She said she knew Stephanie and Dinario, so we interviewed her.

"Dinario Jones told me over the phone that he was on the phone with Stephanie Barron when the murders were happening and that she was scared and crying," she related. The informant swore that Dinario said, "I came to Steph's window about 3:00 a.m. and knocked. I said we need to talk about this so she let me in the back door. The dogs didn't bark because I'd been to the house so many times. Then we went to her room and fucked for awhile." According to the statement, Jones showed Stephanie his .38. He said, "Let's do this," and he held a gun to Stephanie's head and made her kill her parents "for the insurance money."

Here's the problem: we gotta sort the shit from the Shinola. That's shoe polish, by the way. That information from the inmate just didn't pan out. We couldn't prove any of it. We considered it another case of jail talk, and a judge would have called it hearsay.

Writing a statement for Joe Rasco, Monica Chiles, a childhood friend, mentioned that she had known Stephanie Barron since kindergarten. They were close until the eighth grade when Monica started home schooling. Although they lost touch, Monica knew Stephanie had started to date blacks, and her folks didn't like it. Apparently she wanted to marry one that she dated for two years. The summer of 1998, Stephanie and Monica got back in touch with each other through a mutual friend. But according to Monica, Stephanie was not the same person. She was into drugs and drinking a lot.

Stephanie told her she had sex with many different partners and planned to marry one young man because she wanted to have a baby. On several occasions she believed she might be pregnant but had no idea who the father might be. Stephanie's boyfriend got sent to the Texas Youth Commission, and after that, she met Dinario. Chiles wrote that Barron and Jones were sexually active, and they would buy drugs, use, and sell them. They carried guns. Chiles was at Stephanie's house once when Stephanie said she would kill her mother after her mother asked her to do something. Stephanie said, "I'll kill you, bitch." That's pretty hard core. I'll bet Carla didn't tell Stephen about that.

Kids these days learn code switching when they talk and role switching when they're around certain people. It may be a normal thing now, but I just don't think we were that devious when we were teenagers. Then again, our memories are kind to us when we get older. Hell, I'll say this with certainty, if one of my boys talked to their momma like that, they'd have an ass whippin' coming if I found out.

In written testimony, Mrs. Chiles, Monica's mother, stated, "As far as I know, Stephanie had a good relationship with her parents. Yes, she got mad at them for grounding her. But it wasn't hate. Any teenage kid is going to get mad. She quit school to be with her mother. She was going to college. She was going to marry Dinario, and he was going in the U.S. Army while she was in school. They seemed to have everything worked out. I was very shocked when I found out what happened to her parents. Stephanie is a sweet girl, and I don't believe she did something like that. My daughter has told me many times how sweet and caring Stephanie is, how she is respectful and comes home before her curfew. When she came to our house, she checked in with her mom. If Stephanie got her mom's pager instead of Carla, she got worried about her mom."

Bullshit. I think Monica and her mother need to get on the same page and level with each other. Stephanie showed two different sides of herself, depending on the situation. Just like a psychopath.

We interviewed another former friend Stephanie met at Tyler East Kingdom Hall of Jehovah's Witnesses. The friend wrote that she met Stephanie in middle school, and they became best friends. She spent the night at the Barron home, sometimes the entire weekend, and in her words became an "extra addition to the family" for about two and a half years. Then Stephanie started drinking a lot and using drugs with a new group of high-school friends. "A dark side came out," the friend wrote. When Stephanie said she wished something bad would happen to her parents, the friend became concerned. Barron later said she wished her parents were dead so she could have her mother's truck and the house. This happened following an argument with her folks.

One night Stephanie called her friend. Barron was crying and told her that her dad had thrown her on her bed and shaken her by the shoulders and yelled at her. He'd found out she was dating blacks. He was furious that she was having sex. Mr. Barron apparently said, "I wish you would grow up. I think you're smoking dope. I just wish you would move the hell out of my house." She also said that Stephanie hated her parents and that she would do what she wanted to do. Stephanie apparently said, "If this shit don't stop, I'm going to kill them." The friend said, "You can't mean it, you're just mad." And Stephanie said, "Oh, but I do mean it." The two girls went their separate ways at the friend's request. Probably a good idea.

# CHAPTER FOURTEEN

## D. J. Goes to Jail

**January 12, 2000**

Stand up!" Detective Jim Gholston pats Dinario Jones down and finds a loaded 9 mm gun in the waistband of his sweatpants. Rasco looks a little pensive, a little nervous, a little angry since he has been alone with Jones long enough for the young man to have easily killed him.

Detectives Rasco and Gholston have taken Dinario Jones out of school at 1:30 in the afternoon for interrogation. Jones does not like the detectives; the feeling is mutual. During the interview, Rasco and Gholston ask Jones several times about weapons and, in particular, about giving Stephanie Barron a gun. He denies doing so. In the small interview room at the sheriff's headquarters, Jones slouches in his chair. It is part of the arrogant act of a gang banger.

The interview is not going well. After futile attempts to get the unresponsive Jones to talk, Gholston jumps up and says, "I've had enough of this!" He slams the door on his way across the hall to detective Charles Baker's office. Sometimes an abrupt change of pace turns an interview around. Rasco is by himself with Jones for about thirty seconds. Baker casually asks Gholston if the suspect has been frisked. That was when the detective found the 9 mm gun. They immediately handcuff Jones and arrest him for possession of a firearm in a prohibited place and for theft. Jones's gun had been stolen in a recent burglary. His attitude does not improve. He remains unresponsive; his scowl is permanent. Jones spends a day in jail before making bond.

Two days later, Joe Rasco picks up Jones for the second time at his mother's residence. They travel downtown to Elm Street where Rasco pulls into the salley port at the back of the Smith County Jail. The salley port leads into a secured area. At this point, any officer or detective carrying a weapon must either lock it in the car's trunk or place it in a nearby lockbox. Every male and female who has been arrested enters here to be booked into jail.

After punching in a code and looking into the security camera, Rasco escorts Jones through the electronically controlled door. They walk a short distance and enter through another locked door operated by a jailer, called the first floor picket, who works behind a tinted-glass window.

Those who have been arrested are classified according to the charges. The hard-core murderers, rapists, and arsonists are separated from the low-risk criminals, those arrested for DWI, theft, and misdemeanors. Jones is charged with arson based on information from the interview with John Sneed.

## NO CIVILIANS ALLOWED.

The sign is as visually direct as the loud sound of finality the doors make as they close behind them. After frisking Jones again, Rasco deposits the rubber gloves into the wastebasket and walks with Jones past the holding tanks full of young men arrested for drunkenness and disorderly conduct of some kind. Predictably, they do not look happy; this is not a motel. They stare at Rasco with eyes that have no life, eyes that hold no emotion, not even anger. Rasco ignores them. Jones makes eye contact with a couple of them then slowly looks away. The inmates continue to stare.

## PLEASE HANDCUFF PRISONERS TO BENCH.

All persons brought in for booking sit on a bench looking across at their jailers, who process information in a darkened room in the center of the area. The room has three walls of half-shut windows. These jailers, one at each of three computers, perform the official paperwork, which is sent to a main computer. In five minutes the procedure is complete, if the prisoner is cooperative. The questions are the same and are governed by law. The officers in the picket room can book three people in at a time. On a normal day they handle ten or twelve bookings; on the weekend the number escalates to one hundred. Jones is fingerprinted by a scanning device hooked to another computer. He walks a few feet to his right and is told to sit on a stool in a small, white room for his mug shot.

All prisoners are allowed two phone calls. Jones declines. Rasco takes him down to the first floor and through the Tunnel, a long, dim, concrete underground hallway that connects to the second floor of the Smith County Courthouse by a small elevator. The short hallway to the Tunnel turns at a 45-degree angle with five steps down, seven steps up about midway through the Tunnel, then twelve steps up to a left turn before the final fourteen steps to the subterranean entrance to the courthouse. This is where Jones meets with a magistrate and is "warned," arraigned, and Mirandized again.

Many arresting officers have had to call for assistance to subdue angry prisoners who return from court through the Tunnel. The prisoners seem to know the distance between the security cameras and the alarm switches because fights often occur when the officer is farthest from the four panic buttons. The buttons signal a code red for immediate assistance in the Tunnel. Dinario Jones causes no problems.

## INMATES FACE THIS WALL.

The words stare Jones in the face as he and Rasco take the large elevator to the second-floor picket station where officers monitor all hallways, cell doors, and cells on a four-by-five-foot control panel. Each cell has an intercom.

"Gimme my goddamn medicine, you goddamn assholes! You keepin' it fum me!"

The officers respond to every request, but this is another time when an inmate is more than a little confused. There are twelve main cells in cell block C for killers and others who have been isolated and charged with a violent crime. They await their fate behind massive, metal, red cell doors with a square, five-by-seven-inch window for viewing, covered by a small hinged door with a large lock. Another locked rectangular opening stands about knee-high and is used for food and phone calls. The phones are on rollers. Dinario Jones is led past a cell where a female says over and over, "Pray for me! Please! Pray for me!"

After booking, Jones is interrogated. He sits in front of Rasco, Sheriff Smith, and fire marshall Woody McFarland.

"You tell me dat three people have say that I tol' dem I broke into a house and stole some stuff and set the house on fire."

"Yes, that is correct." Rasco looks straight at Jones. "Are you ready to tell us about what happened on October 25,

1999?"

"Yeah. I done it. I set dat fire. But I did not kill dat little girl and her mother next door on purpose. I only wanted to hide any evidence of the burglary."

The sheriff leans forward and asks, "Did you have any special reason for doing this?"

"Well, a few months ago, I needed some money 'cause I didn't get any for my birthday. I never get nothin' for my birthday. So I start walking down the street to a friend of mine house. He lives by Moore Middle School. So I walk by the house at the corner of Don Street and Blackwell Street, 'bout one block from my house. I saw that no one was at home. I went into the carport and kicked the back door open."

"What time was this?"

"It was real late at night. After midnight."

Rasco asks, "Then what did you do?"

"After I kick the door in, I come back about thirty minutes later, after I walk to the Food Fast on Front Street, you know. I walk back and went in through the door I kicked in. I went into the bedroom and got some jewelry off the dresser and put it in my pocket. I also got a TV off the dresser. I took that stuff to my house and put it in some bushes near my backyard."

"When did you go back?"

"I went back right away. Thas when I seen a pistol in a box at the head of the bed. The pistol was black with wood-grain handles. I grab the gun and then got the CD player out of

142

the living room. I put the gun and CD player where I put the jewelry and TV."

McFarland asks, "Is that when you set the fire?"

"Yeah. Before I left the house with the CD player and gun, I went back to the bedroom and set the bed on fire with my lighter. I furse lit the sheet on the bed by the window and then lit it on the other side. Then I left. I really didn't know if the fire would do anything 'cause it was small when I left."

"Then what happened?"

"Well, I went home and went to sleep and my aunt woke me up a little later and tol' me dat firemen and police was outside and a house was on fire. I went out to the garage and watched a little while."

The interviewers pause to let all this soak in and let Jones think. Finally, Fire Marshall McFarland asks, "Did you get closer to the fire?"

"Yeah, I rode my bike down there. I saw the fire trucks and ambulances. Das 'bout it."

"What happened to the items you stole?"

"'Bout the middle of the morning my girlfriend, Stephanie Barron, came to pick me up at my house. I put all the stuff in the trunk of her car."

"What about the gun?"

"I put dat in the trunk too. We went to Eastwood 'partments, Highway 64. Das when Stephanie saw a white guy she knew walking 'cross the parking lot. She say he has a truck but his mother won't let him drive it. I done know why. Anyway, she call him over to the car. Stephanie ax him if he want to buy the gun. He bought it for $150."

Sheriff Smith steps in. "Let me get this straight. You say that Stephanie Barron sold the gun to a white kid, the gun you stole from the Blackwell house?"

"Yeah, thas right, Mr. Shurff. Then Stephanie and I rode around trying to sell the rest of the stuff on Paluxy Street at some 'partments. We went to a big black dude's place. I done know his name. Anyway, I sold him the television and CD player for fity bucks."

"What about the jewelry?"

"I gave it to Stephanie and another girl. The rings were girl things. I didn't fin' out 'bout people dyin' in the fire 'til later. I saw on the news that it was the home next door to the one I broke in and set on fire."

Deputies escort Jones back to his cell. In the sheriff's office, Rasco says, "Dinario is gonna be officially charged with two counts of murder and arson after that confession."

"Yep. Deputies found a gold ring with two small stones and the necklace in Stephanie's bedroom. They found another gold wedding ring on his other girlfriend's finger. That boy can't keep his pants on. How does he keep up with all these damn girlfriends."

"Beats me, Sheriff. Looks like Jones gave girls the stolen rings as if he married them."

"Yep."

In November 2000, Dinario Jones was convicted and sentenced to seventy years in prison. He is serving time in the Telford Unit outside of New Boston, Texas. There were no charges brought against him in connection with the Barron murders. No concrete evidence was presented to prove that he gave the murder weapon to Stephanie. His sworn statement that Stephanie sold the gun to a sixteen-year-old was untrue.

# Part III
# FEBRUARY: PRETRIAL EVENTS

# CHAPTER FIFTEEN

## The Sheriff and District Attorney:
## The State's Case

J ack, are you ready for some football?"

"You mean the courtroom kind? Yes, sir, Sheriff. We're ready. But I'd sure like to have more solid evidence on ballistics before we go to trial."

District Attorney Jack Skeen filed capital murder charges against Stephanie Barron. Charges are based on proof and intent that connect the suspect to the alleged crime. The DA has a duty to society to prosecute. Also, he has a duty to the accused, especially in the case of young Stephanie, who will be tried as an adult. Skeen decides on who will or will not be charged, the level of the charge, and length of incarceration. This is usually done behind closed doors. Formal charges aren't subject to external review or reversal by anyone. In other words, he's mighty damn powerful.

"Sheriff, how many times have we been here in your office and talked about crime in Smith County?"

"Too many. I catch 'em and put 'em in my jail. You file charges. Hell, the pretrial charges alone are plain embarrassing. Your neighbors read about you in the legal news. You been Smith County's district attorney since 1983. That's a long time, Jack."

"Yeah, we've prosecuted several death penalty cases. Now we've got the Barron trial coming up."

"You know, I may hold the keys to the jail, but you're the gatekeeper to the jailhouse door."

"I like that." Skeen grins. "Gatekeeper."

"I think the Barron deaths were planned as opposed to a crime of passion. Either way, it doesn't make it any easier to understand why people kill each other."

"That's right, Sheriff. And it makes a case like this more complicated because a devious mind is trying to outwit the law."

"There's no doubt that Stephanie Barron was involved in her parents' murders on Christmas morning, but we need good evidence to get a conviction."

"Stephanie Barron's attorneys will consider the significance of every piece of evidence and assign what's called a 'probative value.'"

"A what?"

"Well, the value of the evidence proves or disproves a crime has been committed. Or that the defendant was the one who committed the crime."

"Based on what I've seen, I think Stephanie murdered her parents. With or without the help of her boyfriend, Dinario Jones. It's a done deal."

"But we've got to prove it beyond a reasonable doubt."

"I know. Made any connections to Dinario in the Barron murders?"

"No, but we've got him on the other murder charges already. As far as the Barron case, we'll imply to the judge and jury that the events occurred the way we think they did. It's all about connections. Connecting physical evidence to the perpetrator."

"So where do we stand?"

"Sheriff, all the evidence, the weapon, the piece of latex glove, and the clothing, was found in Stephanie's closet. And we know she was there at the scene. So most of the case is gonna hang on that."

"Yep. We compared the blood spots on the clothing with the murdered parents, the daughter, and the boyfriend. The blood matched only Stephanie."

"Sheriff, did you know we received some information that the daughter might have been involved in a fight with someone the night of the murder?"

"Seems like I read that in a written statement from one of Stephanie's friends. If that were true, the fight could have been with Dinario."

"Yes, that would have placed him at the murder scene. So the blood on her shirt could have been from a fight with Jones. That's a possibility. It's tougher when you don't have eye witnesses or a voluntary, recorded confession. We do know that Stephanie ran down the hallway and locked herself in the bathroom during the initial interview that morning. She probably washed her hands in there. We can present that as a deliberate ploy to wash gunpowder residue off her hands. That sounds good. A deliberate ploy."

"I recall Rasco telling me that she acted funny. That was when Detective Cox explained to her what the AAA kit would indicate on her hands. Cox followed her and listened at the bathroom door. Said it sounded like she was throwing up. Rasco had to ask the grandmother, Mrs. Toner, to unlock the door."

"Depending on the judge, a deliberate ploy is usually admissible. We'll see. Her attorneys will challenge that, but we've got precedence on our side."

"Challenge a deliberate ploy? That ole hound won't hunt. Skeen, if things go our way, Stephanie'll go to prison for a long time."

"Maybe for life. She'll have to serve at least forty years of that because she used a deadly weapon."

"Agent Millslagle found that in her closet."

"Right. She'll get credit for time she's already served. Say

Sheriff, get this. In 1963 this fella Alford was indicted for first-degree murder in North Carolina. There was overwhelming evidence of guilt. His attorney recommended that he plead guilty. The prosecutor agreed to accept a plea of guilty to a charge of second-degree murder. So Alford pled guilty to the reduced charge. But he took the stand and stated that he had not committed the murder. He said he was pleading guilty because he faced the threat of the death penalty if he didn't. Wonder if Stephanie Barron would do that?"

"Hell if I know, Mr. District Attorney. I ain't no lawyer. But she's guilty as sin or I'm not the damn sheriff of Smith County."

"Wonder if she's covering up for Dinario Jones?"

"We may never know, Jack, especially if there's a plea bargain. 'Course she'll have to fess up to avoid a life sentence."

"Right. A lot more than a forgery confession. That charge is still on the books and may come up at the trial."

"Mr. DA, it's nearly showtime. All the major actors are gonna meet in the courtroom. Yep. This is gonna be interesting. I hope this'll be the final pretrial meeting."

"We need to get this show on the road. I've seen public defenders get penalized for letting a backlog of cases build up. And I've seen them rewarded for pushing cases through the courts. I don't mean lawyers would give inadequate defense for the sake of time. I just mean a capital murder trial can take a long time. That's why so many cases go to plea bargaining. Most judges like that. It's quicker. Another reason is that the defendant expects something in return for a guilty plea. Prosecutors are the same way. They can be rewarded when they don't engage in delaying tactics."

"Sheriff, I'm convinced that Jones was involved in the murder. Besides, Stephanie Barron had no experience as far as attaching the laser sight to the gun. And the murders were a planned event. It's not just that she was mad at her parents that night for grounding her."

"You don't think that served as a trigger? You know, something that set her off and her psychopathic side took over? That played a part, don't you think?"

"Yes, I suppose so, but she's being tried for murder, not for being a psychopath. I agree that if she is a psychopath, she was going to kill her parents sooner or later. Stephanie and Dinario probably schemed to get the insurance money. It just happened to be Christmas morning. We're still in the discovery period, Sheriff. Both sides are exchanging information about the case. The Constitution has mandated that. We have to disclose to defense counsel any evidence against their defendant."

"Everything? Hell, how do you ever win a case when the defense knows everything? Smells like roadkill to me."

"I know. We don't have to tell them about our strategy. Or private investigation reports or the list of witnesses in the order they'll be called. But nobody wants any surprises."

"We're assuming that four bullets were discharged from the same weapon. Three hit their targets."

"Yes. But we need ironclad connections between the gun, the shooter, and the bullets, Sheriff."

"You don't carry a gun, but I do. When a shooter cocks the hammer on a revolver, the cylinder rotates. Examining cylinder rotation in a weapon is important, Jack, and rifling could be the key in our case. Rifling is the grooves made inside the barrel of each gun when it is manufactured, which becomes the bullet's signature after firing. Rarely are signatures identical from different guns."

"So we've got to connect the bullets to the gun used in the murders."

On March 6, the court appointed counsel for the defense. Judge Gohmert set the first pretrial hearing for April 3 at 8:30 a.m. But after much legal sashayin', the hearing actually occurred on May 19 when David Dobbs and Jennifer Earls appeared for the state. They requested the trial be set for September. So much for the speedy trial the defense asked for. In the period between the arraignment and the beginning of a trial, both sides typically file so many damn pretrial motions it takes the patience of Job to endure.

Jack called around the middle of May to say he hadn't decided to seek the death penalty. He knows to keep his cards close to his vest. He waited until August to reveal that the state had agreed to waive the death penalty. Some criminals deserve to die because of what they've done to innocent people, but that's not my call. I do think others should be locked up for life because they're a danger to society. People who break the law and are found guilty should be punished according to the crime. As we say in Texas, you live by the gun, you die by the gun.

Toward the end of September, both sides were finally ready for the trial, but they asked the court to extend the pretrial discovery period because of possible new evidence. Judge Gohmert agreed and set the next hearing for October 3.

So now we were in October, and Stephanie Barron had been in jail awaiting trial for about 260 days. She's about to get her day in court, as the saying goes. Both sides were ready to go to trial in the case of the *State of Texas v. Stephanie Barron*. Jury selection was scheduled for Thursday, October 5.

No one but Stephanie Barron knew exactly what caused her to go from an honor student to a gang member's girlfriend. And most likely to a killer. We figured the defense attorneys would call expert witnesses to testify that Stephanie, being so young and all, was not intellectually or mentally capable of committing such a terrible crime. Of course, we thought that was utter bullshit, but that's just the way the advocacy system works.

Her transformation could have been from the things that go along with gangs. Excitement, protection, a socialization of sorts, or drugs. Or it could be that her parents inadvertently pushed her in that direction by telling her who she could not date. We know they ordered her to close her checking account and grounded her. I'm not saying they were bad parents, but their daughter rebelled against her father's authority. And authority must be used wisely. I'm aware of only one incident of physical abuse in the family, when Mr. Barron apparently confronted his daughter by yelling at her and shaking her by the shoulders. From what I can tell, Mr. Barron was trying to do the right thing: scare some sense into her. However, Stephanie did the wrong thing. She didn't respond the way we hope our kids will.

These days, physical abuse goes by different names, depending on who you talk to. I believe in spanking, but some people consider that abusive. That's why the good Lord put that padding back there. So it won't injure a kid when he gets a lickin' he deserves. Might bruise some, but it's not gonna put anybody in the hospital if you do it right. I'm not talking about laying the wood to a little fella. Hell, that's excessive. But some explanation beforehand and a little reinforcement in the end, so to speak, is not a bad thing when it's used the right way.

# CHAPTER SIXTEEN

## Cell Mate Jean Thompson

**7:05 p.m.**

ome with me." According to protocol, no one speaks
to prisoners except to give directions. Deputy Bobby
Garmon places Stephanie Barron in handcuffs behind her
back and secures her cell. He escorts her to the first-floor
interview room.

"Where am I going?"

Garmon does not reply.

"Are you going to search my cell?"

Garmon directs Barron to the interview room across from
the first-floor picket. This is to prevent her from destroying
any evidence, including notes believed to be in her cell and
to gain information from Barron's cell mate. Barron has been
here before. Garmon motions toward a chair. He responds

silently to a question when Barron asks, "Can you move these handcuffs to the front?" He does. The deputy notices her eyes glistening. It is the first emotional response Stephanie Barron has offered in front of anyone.

"Why are you doing this to me?" The question to Officer Garmon sounds as though it comes from a victim. "Are they searching my cell?" She asks this many times.

No response.

Barron becomes progressively more defensive and in an angry tone asks, "Don't you have to have a warrant to search my cell?" When it is clear that she will get no reply from the officer, she starts to cry for the first time.

### 7:15 p.m.

Lieutenant Mike Lusk calls Garmon out of the room and advises him that he is needed at the district attorney's office to assist with the final preparation of the search warrants. Garmon proceeds to the district attorney's office and meets with Assistant District Attorneys Jennifer Earls and David Dobbs and with Jack Skeen. They ask Garmon to drive to the residence of Judge Cynthia Kent, who thoroughly reviews the search affidavits and issues the sealed warrants for Stephanie Barron and her cell.

While Barron is away from her cell, Rasco talks with Jean Thompson, a female inmate who has known Barron for a long time. Thompson is serving a one-year jail term for felony theft.

"What can you tell me about your conversations with Stephanie Barron? Did she ever mention killing her parents?"

"No, sir. Stephanie never told me she killed her parents, but she said she knew it was going to happen. I ask her if she did it, and she said no, she didn't. I told her she was lying to me, and she got real mad. I ask her if her boyfriend did it, and she said she didn't know who did it. She didn't think her boyfriend actually shot them. I kept asking and got no answer, but I have had experience that when she don't answer a question I ask, then usually she would have done whatever it is I asked about. She was worried about some tests on the gun and clothes and stuff like that, but she didn't seem too concerned about what happened to her parents."

"She showed no remorse?"

"No, sir, she didn't. The only time she ever cried in my presence was when she learned that she might not get the insurance. She wanted out of jail so she could collect on her parents' insurance money, you know. Like maybe the murders were committed because of the insurance. When she found out that she was probably not going to get the money, she got furious and stomped around, yelling and screaming that the money was hers, and they can't do that to her after all she did for her momma. I ask her what she meant by that, and then she got mad and said that she had put up with their shit all this time so she deserved the money. Then I was called out on visitation."

"What happened when you got back to your cell?"

"Well, she was in a mood to talk, and she told me three months before her parents' death that there had been another policy taken out on her dad for $175,000. After that, she didn't say nothin', so I left her alone and talked with a girl in 208. We talked about phone calls and mail being screened, and Stephanie heard that. She got real nervous."

"Did she say anything about calls or mail?"

"No, not really. Just got nervous. I could tell."

"What about the boyfriend?"

"Dinario? Yeah, I did wonder if she might be protecting him, like he may have been the one who killed her parents. Or maybe he was there and helped. I dunno."

"Did she ever say he killed them?"

"No. All I know I overheard when she was talking to another cell mate. But the night before her parents' funeral I was talking to her about the deaths and that she needed to tell if she was covering for someone. I ask her if she realized that if she was found guilty she could be given the death penalty. That she did not want to die for someone else, you know. Then she said she thought that her boyfriend might have done it."

"So it could have been both of them."

"Yes, I guess so. She did give me four or five letters to mail to her boyfriend. I read them. In one of the letters she talked about her and Dinario as Bonnie and Clyde, you know, the bank robbers, and when they got the insurance money, they would be Bonnie and Clyde with lots of money and raise hell. But like I said she got real upset when she found out she was getting no insurance money from the policies. Stephanie believed she deserved it. She got upset again when she found out that her letters could be read before they were mailed, but she didn't say what was in the letters. 'Course I knew."

"How did she act when you mentioned her parents and the funeral?"

"Well, that was a while back, but I ask her did she miss her parents and she said yeah, a little. The day of the funeral, she wanted to talk as soon as I woke up. I ask her if she remembered that today was the funeral. She said yeah, but she couldn't go anyway, so who cares. She was all of a sudden happy because she had just gotten off the phone with her boyfriend. She said that he told her she would be getting the insurance money after all and that she was fixin' to go home. She was happier about the money than she was about going home. I don't know where Dinario got that information. He's a damn liar, anyway. But she believes anything he says and was happy and showed no signs of grief. And her parents were the most loving parents a kid could have. I ask her did she love her parents, and she said, yeah, she guessed so."

"Did she say anything else about the murders?"

"I knew that the laws found a bloody sweatshirt and a gun in her closet, so I ask her how did that get there? She gave me a really lame excuse. Said she didn't know. I told her that I knew that she had a part in all this, that she may not have shot them, but she had something to do with it. She didn't say nothin'. I gave her the benefit of doubt and ask if she went in and touched her parents to get the blood on her shirt, and was that when she saw the gun and put the shirt and the gun in her closet. Because she was scared and all. She said no. The only thing she ever wanted to talk about was the money. She loves money. She still writing back and forth to Dinario, and I'm the one that's the go-between."

"Get me those letters if you can. Go with Officer Dixon. Now. We don't have much time."

"Yes, sir, I'll try to find those letters."

### 8:45 p.m.

Garmon returns and takes Stephanie Barron to the property room at the jail.

"What are you going to do to me?"

"I have a warrant for a body search." He shows Barron the warrants for the body search and for her cell. Her 4'11" frame visibly sags. Garmon instructs Dixon to strip search the girl and recover anything that she may be concealing.

Inmate Thompson finds the letters in Stephanie Barron's cell and takes them to Detective Rasco. She relates that she recently copied a note word for word as Stephanie wrote it. "I think the note is in her bra. Stephanie didn't want the note to be a written confession in her handwriting. She flushed her original copy down the toilet."

Thompson states that the note lists all the events that occurred the morning of December 25. Barron asked Thompson to recopy the note in her handwriting "so the laws wouldn't catch it." After reading the original written by Stephanie, Thompson wants the detectives to have the information because she is losing sleep and having nightmares about the contents of the note.

Before Thompson returns to her cell, she tells Rasco that Barron approached her and requested help in coming up with a plan of how the double murder took place so Stephanie could implicate Jones. Barron told her cell mate that the night of the murders she was in her room when Dinario knocked on her window. Stephanie let him inside. She said he pulled his shirt up to show her the murder weapon and said, "We gonna do this."

"What else did she tell you?"

"Stephanie was worried Dinario would testify against her. That's why she wanted to involve him."

"She didn't actually say that Jones shot her parents?"

"That's right."

**9:00 p.m.**

Rasco pours a cup of coffee and props his feet on the corner of his desk. Most of the envelopes show the acronym

*SWAK*, and Barron has written that it means "Sealed with a Kiss." *How unbearably high school,* Rasco thinks. The letters are explicit, vulgar, and sexual in nature. Rasco reads that Stephanie Barron is extremely concerned that Dinario Jones will tell about the letters and testify against Stephanie to gain some advantage concerning his own situation.

*That must be why she needs a plan to involve her boyfriend in the murders. She's afraid of Dinario. The letters got here anyway,* Rasco surmises.

The handwriting varies somewhat from letter to letter; she is trying to disguise her writing, but it is an amateurish, although devious, effort. He reads on. "Sorry if my hand-writing is fucked up, I'm trying to change my shit up so the laws won't recognize it—hopefully."

She also explains she is using false names or names of other people in the jail. The more Rasco reads, the more he thinks these are typical thug love notes and are somewhat incriminating.

## Evidence Marked 04-5-2000

"Oh get this bullshit—I don't have any lawyers right now. Know why? B/C that bitch you was talking to made a statement against me and those were her lawyers too. So I want you to know, if you hadn't been talking to her I would still have a chance. Now, I done lost 2 of the best lawyers there was—thanks asshole.

I dare one of these hoez to run up on me right now. I am not starting nothing but I'll damn sure finish it. But all this extra bullshit is startin' to get to me."

## Marked 05-19-2000

"I guess you saw me on the news last night, and on the front page with a full-size color picture. I had to dress pimp for court. I musta set off the fire alarm. They sayin I aint got too good of a chance. They keep tryin to get me to tell them you was there at my house on Christmas, but I aint gonna. My investigator was tryin to get crunk with me the other day. My date is Sept 14 and I go for another pretrial in the middle of August. I'm gonna see if I can dress out in real clothes again for that pretrial. I already know I'm gonna get some time regardless, so fuck it."

## Marked 06-07-2000

"Baby, these white folks is not playin with us. I done know if I'm even gonna take this to trial or not yet. They still considering the death penalty for my ass. I'm gonna be spending the rest of my life locked up, and you gonna be out eventually. You done give a damn, all you worried about is yourself, and yes there are tears on this paper. You have no idea what I'm going through. Hell, I still take up for your ass when these hoez started in about the car, and how you signed the confession. These fuckin hoez are all worried about our business when they need to be worried about they damn self. Cuz they aint getting shit out of me. And hear this, I got folks I done even know writin shit on me. Some lady at R.E.L. high school said a girl was cryin about some shit about you and her. I already know that hoe was lying. I know those statements aint true, but shit, its our word against theirs. And another thing, so you sayin I aint your wife no more? That's fucked off. I was really believing you loved me cuz you give me that ring with two diamonds. I aint tryin to put my shit on you. You already got 2 murders of your own. I got an idea though. Why the fuck you gotta cuss at me so much. I told you I wasnt trying to say you was there at my house Christmas morning."

### Marked 06-21-2000

"I found out today about the lawsuit shit that they gone put the $ to the court for them to decide whether I get convicted or not. So apparently we aint got the insurance $ yet. You said we would. I guess the $ to pay the bills and shit came out of a different policy. So, I aint gotta worry bout that right now."

### Marked 06-24-2000

"I aint gone plead out—I done think. I seen in the paper where my attorney is actin' bad on another case he's repre-senting. So that's a good sign for me. I might beat this rap-shit."

## Cell Mate Jean Thompson

**Marked 06-29-2000**

"Yea—in a way I wish I was pregnant, but that would add on to the stress I already got. Besides, they already tryin to use that as a motive and if I really was, I would've been fucked. Hell, yo ass was too scary to leave it in and nut inside me. I wanted you to, but you was always too scared. I know we'd be able to now, you aint smoked kill for awhile. I aint gone plea out, now that I see my lawyer is doing good in court—that makes me feel better."

**Marked 07-17-2000**

"I'm fucked if the DA's get a hold of my letters, especially when I am not supposed to even be writing you."

**Marked 07-27-2000**

"Hey baby. Get this. These hoez stare at my ass the whole time we on the damn roof for rec. They be peepin me. They all straight line ass hatas. You know baby, I done think they got shit to convict me on. They aint came at me with no numbers. I aint takin no plea no ways. I aint no muthafuckin hata, but I damn sure done cut for no law. I been on top of my game. So what's the plea they tryin to give you—I know what they tryin to do—I'm not stupid. You gone get your letters in your cellie's name. Fuck the letter shit and fuck the laws. I done give a fuck. And I didn't say I was gone quit writing you. I said I done need the laws getting my shit. I'm fixin to go to sleep—I been up way too long clownin on these hoez that are trying to bulldyke."

## Marked 8-30-2000

"I guess I'm gone have to tell my lawyers what really happened to my parents especially if they readin my mail. I'm fucked I think."

Rasco picks up the note that was recovered from Stephanie's bra during the strip search.

## 2:00 a.m. Christmas morning.

I woke up around 2 a.m. and got dressed. I walked back and forth between my room and my parents' room for about two hours. I wore latex gloves and held a gun the whole time. Around 4 a.m. I finally went into their bathroom and held the gun up, then lowered it. I closed the lid on the toilet and sat down, and it was like I heard Dinario's voice saying "Do it. Do it." I thought about all the good times we had as a family, but then I heard my dad yelling at me. I walked into their bedroom at 4:04 a.m. and told myself to do it, but I couldn't. I went back to the toilet seat and sat there. I returned to their bedroom, and this time I held the gun up and pushed the infrared on. I positioned the dot on my dad and held it til the clock read 4:08. I closed my eyes and pulled the trigger and shot him in the back of the neck, then held it to my mom. She sat up, and

# Cell Mate Jean Thompson

I shot her in her face. The infrared fell off, and I dropped the gun. I ran and turned on the bathroom lights. I saw my dad stumbling around so I picked up the gun and put the beam in my pocket. I shot my dad again, but missed, and then I was just shooting, and I shot my mom in the arm. I pulled my parents' dresser drawers out, ran back to my room, and got some pliers. I ran outside and cut my telephone wires and ran around the corner and fell in some stickers. I was running in my socks. I ran back into the house and to my room. I grabbed my stereo and threw it in my closet then pulled my clothes off and stuffed them and the pliers in the very bottom of the hamper. I threw the sweat pants and top in the basket with the gun in the front pocket. Then I ran next door.

Timing is everything. Finding the notes and this copy of the letter apparently written by Stephanie is almost serendipity, if Rasco believed in that sort of thing. If it were in her handwriting, it would be solid evidence. *The pieces may be coming together*, Rasco thinks.

The note clearly contains a detail only the shooter would know: shooting the father first in the back of the neck. The note is far different from the letters. Her high school English essays were probably a far cry from the street-talking, thug-love letters to Dinario Jones.

Rasco rereads the statement from Jean Thompson: "I asked her if she had gotten into a bad argument with her parents the night of the murders. She said no, they just grounded her for not having closed her checking account and she was real pissed."

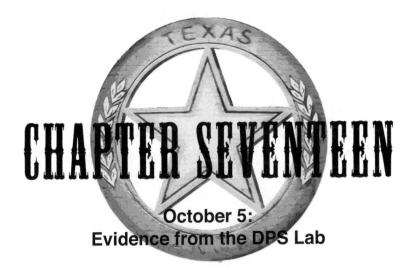

# CHAPTER SEVENTEEN

## October 5:
## Evidence from the DPS Lab

The district attorney called to say that the jury was scheduled to be picked for the Stephanie Barron capital murder trial on October 3. But the case turned our way before it went to a jury. Rasco received a package from the Department of Public Safety lab just in time. I hate to say it, but it was a little like TV, although our drama would take up the whole season rather than just one episode.

Walking toward the entrance to the courthouse, Rasco takes the three granite steps leading to the glass double doors. The local newspaper's headline in the metal vendor box mentions something about the upcoming Barron murder trial, but Rasco does not stop to read.

He nods to the female security officer standing in front of the security system where everyone other than law enforcement empties their pockets.

"Morning."

"Yes, sir."

The area reminds him of his days in the Air Force and the hundreds of times he observed airport security. As in the military, he waits. Assistant District Attorney David Dobbs appears by Rasco's side.

"Sir, I've got what we need to put this puppy to bed."

"Like what?"

"The definitive ballistics report proving Stephanie Barron's gun was the murder weapon. It's all here. I got it this morning from Garland DPS lab."

"We got 'em."

They proceed to the largest courtroom in the building, the Seventh Judicial District Court. A lighted sign above the entrance shows that court is in session. Rasco grabs a gold handle and pulls the door toward him, holding it open for Dobbs. The two defense attorneys turn and acknowledge Dobbs and Rasco.

The courtroom is a fifties-style stately room with a twenty-five-foot ceiling. Ornately framed pictures of former seventh district judges decorate one wall. The two men pass twelve rows of oak benches separated by an aisle. The empty benches, called the public area, face north toward the judge's chambers and are separated from the area for attorneys, the jury box, and the judge's bench by a five-inch-thick wooden partition that extends the length of the room. A swinging gate in the middle of the partition permits entry and exit.

Assistant District Attorney Jennifer Earls walks toward them. Dobbs turns toward the judge as he enters the courtroom. Ms. Earls looks at Rasco.

"Detective, you look confident this morning."

"Yes, ma'am. We have cause for confidence." He turns his back to the defendant's attorneys and softly says, "About forty-five minutes ago, I received the DPS lab report on the bullets found in Beth Little's house. They are a definite match to the bullets found from Stephanie Barron's gun."

Earls smiles and says nothing but clinches Rasco's arm just above his elbow as a gesture of victory.

Rasco turns back to the defense attorneys who are watching him and says, "Good morning, gentlemen."

There is a reason judges are called "Your Honor." They wield a god-awful amount of decision-making, life-changing power at all phases of criminal proceedings.

The primary responsibility of District Judge Louis Gohmert is to reach a formal legal decision based on presentation of evidence to a jury. The backstage negotiations are over. Preliminary matters are usually settled in the judge's chambers after careful examination of the material and the conditions under which it was obtained. Open court begins in two days if the case goes to trial.

The judge's bench is elevated three feet and is encased in

dark oak. Judge Gohmert moves to the black, high-backed leather chair. The witness stand is to his right. Near the wall-mounted seal of the State of Texas above the chair are the Texas flag and the American flag. A microphone, attached to the railing of the witness stand, points toward a single, gray, cloth-lined witness chair. The view from the gray chair shows the jury box twelve feet away, which has two rows of wooden chairs, graduating in elevation like a movie theater. The show is about to begin.

Everyone is here: Jack Skeen, Assistant District Attorneys David Dobbs and Jennifer Earls, Barron's two defense attorneys, and Stephanie Barron, dressed in a two-piece tan prisoner's jumpsuit. Not very pimp. Mrs. Toner sits quietly in the front row of the public area. If this were the open trial, the area would include the press and television. The benches in the public area would be full.

The prosecution team realizes that Judge Gohmert must consider Stephanie Barron's blameworthiness. He is aware she has been in trouble before so, she has a history, although short. And he will consider the amount of harm she caused her parents if she murdered them in cold blood as the prosecution team is trying to prove. The judge will consider the fact that the defendant used a deadly weapon as well as the implications and impact of sending an eighteen-year-old to prison, although by law she is certified as an adult.

The lead defense lawyer greets everyone: "Good morning,

Mr. Skeen, Ms. Earls, Mr. Dobbs, and Detective Rasco."

The prosecution team does not sit down. They have conversed quietly and decided that Assistant District Attorney Jennifer Earls should break the news.

Skeen says, "Judge, let's get right to it. We've got new information. New discovery."

"A surprise? What's up with that?" The defense attorney interrupts. "We don't know anything about new information. Last week, you came up with a witness who was a cell mate and is going to testify against our client. I thought that was it."

Jennifer Earls steps forward. "That's true. Our informant says Ms. Barron talked to her about the killings and insurance money. We're considering that to be motive. Even Judge Gohmert just found out about this new evidence. Detective Rasco got it about an hour ago."

The two defense attorneys look at each other grimly. They are not pleased with this new turn of events.

"The lab report from the Department of Public Safety clearly states that the bullets fired from the Stephanie Barron gun were from the same lot as the unfired bullets from Beth Little's house where the gun was stolen by Dinario Jones. Jones gave the gun to Barron."

Judge Gohmert intervenes. "Defense, would you like to speak privately with your client?"

Without responding, the two defense attorneys escort their

client away. The next twenty minutes will change Stephanie Barron's life forever.

"Detective Rasco, you've already got the report concerning two of the three fired .38-caliber bullets that had been fired by the pistol belonging to Stephanie Barron."

"That's correct, Mr. Skeen. The third bullet lacked sufficient microscopic detail to be a positive match to the weapon used in the murder."

"So the rifling characteristics of two bullets are consistent with having been fired by the Barron pistol?"

"Absolutely. The report also confirms that the wear marks are due to the laser sight Stephanie apparently attached to the weapon."

"Apparently?"

"Yes, sir. I'm not convinced she knew how to attach the laser sight to the barrel. She had limited knowledge of weapons. Probably had help."

"Rasco, we don't have any evidence to prove that she had help. And Jones goes on trial next month for the murders of Shelley Rae Haynes and her three-year-old daughter, Hannah."

Barron's attorneys explain the new evidence and her options to Stephanie. "Ms. Barron, your chances are 50-50 if we go to trial, 60-40 if the court will consider a plea. The decision is yours."

"Tell me what to do! I don't wanna go to no jail!"

Her attorneys try to calm her and repeat everything she needs to know.

Her defense counsel has been in this situation before because Smith County is known for stern judges and harsh juries. The worst case scenario is ninety-nine years and a $10,000 fine. Stephanie agrees to plea and accepts seventy-five years.

# CHAPTER EIGHTEEN

## Plea and Sentencing

T he defendant will rise."

Stephanie Barron has been sitting between her attorneys at a desk to the judge's left. The defense attorney closest to Judge Gohmert looks toward a dark TV monitor next to a five-drawer filing cabinet. His eyes look dissatisfied. The defendant's puffy face makes her look displaced, like a person who is supposed to be somewhere else. She lists aimlessly to the right a little, like a toy sailboat without a rudder. Her attorney steadies her at her elbow.

Rasco notices the defendant's maternal grandmother, Mrs. Toner, who has attended all of Stephanie's court appearances. She is dressed in a brown outfit, suitable for church. She wears a permanent face of sorrow as she stares at her granddaughter.

After learning of the ballistics report Skeen entered into evidence, Stephanie Barron's attorneys have convinced her that her best course is to plead guilty to two counts of murder. Her guilty plea will save her at least ten years in prison. If convicted by a jury, she would have received what District Attorney Jack Skeen asked for: life behind bars.

All three stand. Stephanie is sobbing. Both attorneys support her as she stands before the judge.

"All right. I've been provided with paperwork in Causes 7-1152-00 and 7-1153-00, *State of Texas v. Stephanie Barron*. In both cases, it's my understanding from the attorneys for both sides that pleas are to be entered."

The judge pauses and looks straight at the young defendant. "Ms. Barron, I know you've been in here for numerous hearings and you understand that before I can accept a plea, I have to make sure you understand what you're doing. That you have a clear mind here today before I can accept it. Raise your right hand."

Stephanie Barron is sworn in and sits down. A deputy places the microphone near so she will be heard, according to the judge's instructions. She scoots her chair closer to the microphone.

Judge Gohmert addresses the state: "It's my understanding that if pleas are entered today, the other charges concerning forgery will be dismissed."

Jennifer Earls stands and states that this is correct.

"All right. Now, Ms. Barron, you understand you're entitled to a trial by jury. You're entitled to proceed with jury selection tomorrow and plead 'not guilty' to the capital murder charge and then see if the state can prove the allegations against you beyond a reasonable doubt. Do you understand?"

"Yes, sir."

"Can you move a little closer to the microphone? Now, by coming in here and pleading guilty in these two cases and stipulating to the evidence, then I can find you guilty and sentence you for a minimum of five years, up to ninety-nine years, or life. You understand that?"

"Yes, sir."

"All right. Now I need to make sure your mind is clear this morning. Have you had anything at all, whether it was cough medicine, anything at all that contained any type of alcohol in the last twenty-four hours?"

"No, sir. I've been in jail."

"I realize that, Ms. Barron. Are you under the influence right now of any type of drug, narcotic, intoxicant, or any kind of medication?"

"No, sir."

"Are you under any kind of physician's care at this time?"

"No, sir."

"Have you ever been confined in a mental institution or under psychiatric care?"

"No, sir."

183

"Can you read, write, and understand English?"

"Yes, sir."

"It's my understanding that in May of this year you turned eighteen. Is that correct?"

"Yes, sir. I was in jail." Stephanie looks at her grandmother, who has her hand over her mouth as if she is trying not to speak. Or cry.

"Right. Now look at state's exhibit 1 for each of the two cases. Is this your signature on exhibit 1?"

"Yes, sir."

"It appears that you have signed several waivers. Let me show you all the pages. Among them are the waivers of trial by jury, new trial motion, and right of appeal. Did you sign each of these documents, each of these pages I've turned through and showed you?"

"Yes, sir, I did."

"Did you read over each page with your attorney and understand each page before you signed it?"

"Yes, I did."

"Any questions?"

"No, sir."

"All right. I know you and your attorneys have spent a lot of time preparing for this case. By waiving the right to have this considered by a jury, and by entering a plea today, you will waive your ten days to prepare for trial and your right to a jury trial. Understand?"

"Yes, sir."

"Now the pending case is one of capital murder. I want you to understand that if we proceeded to trial and the jury found you not guilty, that's the end of it. If we proceeded to trial and they found you guilty of capital murder, then the sentence is automatic life, no eligibility for parole for at least forty years, for a minimum of forty years. So if I go along with all this, by the pleas that have been entered, you'd receive a sentence of seventy-five years in each case, and under that scenario you would not become eligible for parole for at least forty years. Is that the state's understanding?"

Earls responds. "It is, Your Honor."

"And defense's understanding?"

"Yes, that's our understanding."

"All right. Now the agreed recommendation in each of these cases appears to be for seventy-five years in the Texas Department of Criminal Justice Institutional Division and that the court would make an affirmative finding that a deadly weapon was used or exhibited during the course of the offense. Now, you understand I'm not required to go along with these agreed recommendations, but if I sentence you any more harshly than what the state's agreed to recommend, I would give you a chance to withdraw your plea and enter a plea of 'not guilty.' Then we would go ahead with jury selection tomorrow. Understand?"

"Yes, sir."

185

"If I do accept the recommendation and sentence you to seventy-five years in each of these two cases, and if I considered the forgery in sentencing and allowed these two cases to run concurrently, and made the affirmative finding of a deadly weapon in each case, then that would mean I had gone along with the agreed recommendations between you and the state, and you would basically be stuck with that. Understand?"

Although her eyes seem glazed, the defendant answers "Yes, sir." She is lost amid all the legal jargon and does not care anymore. She is thinking about Dinario Jones.

"All right. Very well then. At this time, I need to ask you to stand. I ask you in cause 7-1152-00, in which you are charged with the murder of Stephen Barron by shooting him with a firearm, how do you plead?"

"Guilty."

"I ask you in cause 7-1153-00, in which you are charged with the murder of Carla Barron by shooting her with a firearm, how do you plead?"

Stephanie cannot hear the judge over the voice of Jones saying, "Do it. Do it." Judge Gohmert again says, "How do you plead, Ms. Barron?" She resists her deep desire to plead otherwise and says, "Guilty."

"Ms. Barron, you're pleading guilty because you are guilty; you have not been threatened or coerced. These things alleged are actually true, and this is your own choice?"

"Yes, sir." Dinario speaks to her again, but Stephanie

brushes his voice away.

"All right then. Ms. Barron, based on your pleas and your statements here today, I do find that your pleas are freely, intelligently, knowingly, and voluntarily entered, so I accept your pleas of guilty. Anything further in the way of evidence on either of these cases on guilt or innocence?"

"Not from the state, Your Honor."

"Not from the defense."

"Ms. Barron, you've indicated you are willing to waive the pre-sentence investigation and proceed with sentencing today. Or do you want to wait for a pre-sentence investigation?"

"Today, sir."

Now she hears the voice of her mother. "Stephanie, it's OK." Fighting off a dizzy sensation, she shakes her head in a twitching motion.

Judge Gohmert studies the defendant's face. "Ms. Barron, are you OK?"

"No, sir. Oh. Yes, sir." Her attorneys steady her again.

"Ms. Barron, in cause 7-1152-00, this court finds you guilty of the murder of Stephen Barron as alleged by shooting him with a firearm. I also find that a deadly weapon was used during the course of that offense.

"In cause 7-1153-00, this court finds you guilty of the murder of Carla Barron by shooting her with a firearm and affirmatively find that you used a deadly weapon, a firearm, during that offense as well.

"With regard to the forgery charged in cause 7-41-00, I cannot consider that in sentencing unless there's a judicial confession. You're under oath; do you want me to consider that, Ms. Barron?"

"A confession?" She looks at the lead counsel. He nods. "Yes, sir."

"Are you guilty of that forgery?"

"Yes, sir."

Stephanie Barron is crying. Judge Gohmert looks down at his notes. The state team looks straight ahead, waiting for the judge to announce the sentence after accepting the plea bargain.

"All right. Then I'll consider that and will go along with the agreed recommendations in each of these cases and, accordingly, sentence you to seventy-five years in the Texas Department of Criminal Justice Institution Division on both charges, to run concurrently. And the time that you've been held in jail on these offenses will be applied toward the seventy-five-year sentence in each case."

The judge asks if the state or defense knows of any legal reason why sentencing should not be carried out. They say no.

"Then Ms. Barron, it's the order of this court that you be remanded to the custody of the Smith County sheriff's office and that you be transported to the Texas Department of Criminal Justice Institutional Division to have these two sentences carried out."

Judge Gohmert looks at Stephanie for a moment. "Ms. Barron, you're not going to have anybody there for you when you get out. You know that. Your parents are certainly not going to be there. Your grandmother who has been here, well, there's a good chance she won't be there when you get out."

Stephanie feels her grandmother's eyes on the back of her neck and hears a humming sound that drowns out the voices.

The judge takes a breath and shakes his head. "May God have mercy on your soul. Well then, we'll stand adjourned."

The eighteen-year-old can barely walk through her heaving and the heavy shackles around her ankles. She collapses back into her chair, but her attorneys pry her from her seat. Little Stephanie Barron bends over in convulsions, her forehead resting on the railing. The deputy moves to the edge of his seat. At the judge's signal, the officer escorts Barron from the courtroom to serve out her sentence. Mrs. Toner moves near with her arms stretched out toward Stephanie. The girl raises her cuffed hands together and touches her grandmother. Mrs. Toner cannot believe she is guilty. She will never believe it.

# CHAPTER NINETEEN

## Jakes

Joe Rasco and I rarely celebrate anything. We're too damn busy. But we were so pleased that the Barron case didn't go to trial, we met at Jakes on the square. I invited Jeff Millslagle too.

I like Jakes. It's what I'd call an upscale bar with good food. It's still got the old wood planks on the floor and original iron-ore bricks from the 1880s on the walls. Reminds me of New Orleans.

Rasco ordered two beers at a time and mixed them. He called it a "black and tan." The black was Guinness and the tan was Bass Ale. I remember that because he took a silver spoon out of his shirt pocket. It had a crook in the handle for balancing on the lip of the glass. He poured the Bass, filling the glass a little over half full. Then he tried to layer the Guinness on top by dripping it over the inverted spoon. Didn't work. It all mixed together.

I ordered Crown Royal and Coke.

Rasco wanted to talk about the case.

"You know, Sheriff, there's a long history to parricide, children killing their parents. It's one of mankind's—excuse me—humankind's oldest crimes. Remember Charles Whitman, the mass killer of Austin, Texas?"

"Yes."

"In 1966, he murdered his mother. Stabbed her, shot her in the back of the head. Then he killed his wife. Just awful."

"Yep. How's your beer?"

"Fine. Then Whitman took several weapons to the observation tower at the University in Austin and killed about eleven people. One was pregnant."

"Terrible. How's your family?"

"Fine. You know, Sheriff, it's hard to understand perversity like that. One idea dominates a person's mind. Like Stephanie Barron's. I think she got it in her mind to get that insurance money for her and her boyfriend."

"She was obsessed. I guess her sense of her own importance and purpose just got out of control. She saw no reason why she shouldn't have everything she wanted. The house, the insurance money, the vehicles. And apparently it made sense to her to kill her parents to get it. Weird."

"Evidently."

Jakes

"There's Millslagle."

"Gentlemen, I'm buying."

"I'll have another Crown Royal."

"Am I ever glad that case didn't go to trial. Might have lasted a long time. We'd all be tied up in court right now instead of here at Jakes. Remember that morning in Stephanie's bedroom? I found that gift bag with the hundred-dollar bill. Well, I put a sticky note inside the bag that read 'We found the money.'"

"Is that why I heard her yelling when she came back from her grandmother's house?"

"Yeah. That's when she found my note. She wasn't very happy about that."

"Millslagle, you gotta have a sense of humor in this business. By the way, Rasco, you did a damn fine job on ballistics to bring the pretrial to a close."

"Thanks, Sheriff. But something's starting to bother me."

"About the Barron case? A little late."

"Waiter. Why doesn't the name *Jakes* have an apostrophe indicating possession? You know, *J-a-k-e*-apostrophe-*s*."

"I really don't know, but Rick's here. You can ask him."

"Rasco, Rick and I go back a ways. He serves the best chicken-salad sandwich between Dallas and Shreveport."

"I'd say he's the second most recognized person downtown. Just behind you, Sheriff."

"J. B. How are you?"

"Fine, Rick, fine. Rasco's got a question. Why isn't there an apostrophe in the name *Jakes*?"

"Helluva question. The story I got when I took this place over was that a group of guys owned it originally. It wasn't one Jake but several Jakes, so they voted not to have an apostrophe because of the group ownership. That's all I know."

"Then the apostrophe should be after the '*s*'."

"Let it go, Rasco."

"But Sheriff, if the word *men* is already plural and you want to make it possessive, you add the apostrophe before the final *s*. As in *men's*."

"I'm ignoring that remark. Drink your beer. Thanks, Rick."

"Sheriff, Stephanie Barron had minimal experience with a firearm. I think someone else put that laser sight on the gun."

"Could be. That Jones character knew she was going to kill her parents. You tried your damndest to prove that Jones made an appearance that night. I really believe he at least wanted to help her kill her parents. She talked to Jones that night. Didn't you say you saw his name and number on the caller ID?"

"No, sir. That was someone else's name."

"Rasco, this was a planned event, not a crime of passion or rage. It was clean. Real clean."

"You're probably right. Happened on Christmas Day. She could have been sick and tired of not getting presents like

194

other kids. Money was her motive. She lived in the house; that's the opportunity. She had the gun from Dinario: there's your means. Motive, opportunity, and means."

"Yep. She probably knew good and well she was going to kill her parents while they were sleeping that morning. She had plenty of opportunities to kill them in other situations. She chose Christmas. Psychopaths can fool you. They seem decent on the outside, but inside they're very sick. Sane but sick, if that makes any sense. Hell, psychopaths go by their own rules."

"Remember the statement from the lady who worked with Stephanie Barron at Apple Fitness? Stephanie told her that she was dating a probable gang member who carried a gun. She stole a check from Apple and cashed it for Dinario Jones."

"She got caught and was fired. After that, Barron called the coworker and said she'd blow the place up because she'd been fired. That's kinda sick."

"Yeah, they stole clothes from Dillard's and Foley's. The coworker said that's how they dressed so pimp. That was her word—'pimp.'"

"Millslagle, what do you think?"

"Here's what I remember: Stephanie Barron was unbelievably calm that morning. Her eyes were vacant. A cold fish. If your parents had just been shot, especially on Christmas morning, you might just be a little upset. She wasn't. Unemotional and matter-of-fact about the whole thing.

Sheriff, I thought that morning that Stephanie Barron was our number-one suspect."

"I guess we all did. She was the only one there. At least that's what we thought."

"When I heard her story at her grandmother's house, I was 80 percent sure she did it. Victims usually know the perpetrator. I didn't want to think it because she was a teenager. It took me several days of arm wrestling with myself to really think she was guilty. I had a hard time dealing with that as an investigator and as a parent."

"Sheriff, I recall that morning during the interview, Stephanie started talking about the insurance money. That struck me. Maybe it was as simple as that. She had a car she had to pay off and a boyfriend to keep happy. She needed *denarii* to keep Dinario happy."

"What the hell are you talking about, Rasco?"

"One other thing, Sheriff. If you hear gunshots, you're going to find the quickest way out. The nearest exit. But Stephanie Barron went all the way to the other end of the house when she said there was an intruder. A door was only a few feet from her bedroom."

"Yeah, we shot all kinds of holes through her testimony. Good work. That little girl never considered getting caught. That's a real defect in reasoning. Lines up with a typical psychopath. I've been studying murder and the criminal mind for a long time. I've been responsible for investigating over

140 homicides since 1978. That's a lot for a county this size. Matter of fact, I've probably put more criminals on death row than any sheriff in Texas."

"You ought to be in the *Guinness Book Of World Records*."

"Damn right. I probably am. Listen to that great song. Etta James's 'At Last.' And there's my professor friend dancing with his wife. I love to dance. After my Navy service, I was a very successful dance instructor. You know that, Rasco? Women love a man who can dance."

"Don't have time for that kind of thing, Sheriff."

"Hey, professor! I want to talk to you about writing a book with me. You teach writing and all that. What do ya think?"

"You know what they say, J. B., 'If you can teach it, you can do it.'"

"Uh, Joe, remember that movie about baseball and the line, 'If you build it, they will come'?"

"Yes, sir."

"Have you ever heard the line, 'If you can teach it, you can do it'?"

"No, sir, I don't believe I have."

"Me neither."

"Sheriff, I'm still thinking about why they named this place *Jakes* with no apostrophe."

"Excuse me, detective, but I've got to go to the m-e-n-apostrophe-s room."

"You know, Sheriff, it's hard not to be a pedant."

197

"A what?"

"Pedant. Someone who hits you over the head with a grammar book every time you make a mistake."

"That's better than hittin' you over the head with a Bible every time you make a mistake. Rasco, you stick to crime-scene investigation, and you'll be fine. And I wouldn't worry about takin' dance lessons anytime soon."

"Yes, sir."

# EPILOGUE

From: Steve Roloff
To: Sheriff J. B. Smith
Sent: Saturday, May 1, 2006, 10:35 a.m.

Sheriff Smith,
I am married to Stephanie Barron. A television producer told me you are writing a book about Stephanie's case. Please allow me the opportunity to give you all the facts in this case, as I believe Stephanie to be innocent of killing her parents. I hope you will consider my request before completing your work on this project.

Regards,
Steve Roloff

J. B. don't read no e-mail. But my secretary told me there's something important about this e-mail that I really needed to see. Hell, this book was in the final stages of editing at Brown Books Publishing Group, and I get zapped out of nowhere by Stephanie's husband. I didn't even know she got hitched.

Because of two words in the e-mail, "facts" and "innocent," I talked to Joe Rasco, current District Attorney Matt Bingham, and David Dobbs, who is now in private practice. They all agreed that I should go for it because, as they said, people do get convicted for crimes they don't commit. That usually involves a legal error that must be overturned, eyewitness mistakes, and law enforcement and prosecutorial misconduct. Then there's the problem of inadequate counsel and faulty DNA testing. Frankly, I've never believed we had any of these problems in the Barron case. This new turn of events would have to be about new evidence.

I responded to Roloff because the Texas Constitution gives me the right as Sheriff of Smith County to reopen any case that was adjudicated in my county if there is a compelling reason to do so. New evidence would be a damn-fine reason. If an inmate hires the right lawyer, a prisoner can take his case all the way to the Texas Court of Criminal Appeals and on to the federal court system. That's a lot of expensive real estate to cover, but if you've got the money, honey, some lawyer's got the time.

So I told Roloff I had written a book about Stephanie Barron, and it was about to go to press. But any changes at this point might delay the publication. I also told him he or Stephanie would have to convince me to pursue this or not. I'm a busy man, and I don't have time to chase spider webs in the wind.

May 4, 2006, 12:39 p.m.

Sheriff Smith,
If you should decide not to give me the opportunity to meet with you, let me explain something. A convicted felon who spent time in federal prison for money laundering and fraud convinced Stephanie to plead guilty. Then he collected the insurance money. There is a great deal more to this case than what you read about in the detectives' reports. Please understand that neither me or Stephanie are against you writing on her case. We just would hope you would be fair and tell the truth.

Sincerely,
Steve Roloff

First of all, Roloff seemed like a nice guy, but I wondered right away if what we said in the book was proving itself true right in front of me: Stephanie is a psychopath. In e-mail correspondence with Roloff, I learned that he was crazy in love with Stephanie and had sold his home to raise money for her defense. But I had to ask myself: did she manipulate this young man who had a high-paying management job and convince him to sell his $350,000 home and move into a small $650 apartment? That's the only way he could afford an attorney, who required a $50,000 retainer, for his new wife.

201

Secondly, I was suspicious. But I told him I'd remain open about the case.

Roloff asked that I be fair and tell the truth in the book. I explained to him that this book falls into a certain category, "true crime," which is also called creative nonfiction. I said that the work of many detectives was combined into one person, Joe Rasco. The written testimony was turned into dialogue between Rasco and people who knew Stephanie and her parents, but we changed all the names except Stephanie's and Dinario's. A few situations have been changed or created based on logical leaps from the actual events. That's the way true crime works. If you can't handle that, don't read true crime.

May 7, 2006, 09:17 P.M.

Sheriff Smith,

You asked what it's like to be married to an inmate. And yes, to quote you, I "ain't gettin' any" because the state of Texas does not allow conjugal privileges. Loss of liberty is devastating, but loss of heterosexual relationships is a serious problem. Involuntary celibacy can lead to sexual victimization. A beautiful 18-year-old like Stephanie must have been quite a temptation to some of the more experienced female inmates, but I know she's strong.

I met Stephanie when I was a sales manager at a car dealership in Tyler. I worked out at Apple Fitness where Stephanie was a receptionist and daycare employee

# Epilogue

and got to know her. I could see she was going in the wrong direction. When she started dating Dinario Jones, I saw a definite change in her appearance and attitude.

I moved away, and about a year and a half later I saw Stephanie on E! Entertainment Channel and found out what happened. The show was about women behind bars or something like that. I wrote to her, and she responded: "I didn't do it!" were her first words to me. After three months she started talking about the murders. You may know this, but the blood found on her shirt was on her nightshirt, and she had nosebleeds. The blood was hers, her fingerprints were not on the gun, Dinario's gun, and the tests that were done that day found no evidence of gunpowder residue on her hands. She swore to me she never washed her hands that morning. She says the so-called jailhouse confession found in her bra was somehow planted. They used that against Stephanie to force her to plea bargain. My wife was a seventeen-year-old child with no parents, a step-grandfather she could not depend on, and she was forced to make a decision in about twenty minutes that would affect the rest of her life. My wife may be guilty of being stupid, of lying and being immoral, but she's not a murderer.

Sincerely,
Steve Roloff

I agree with one thing: she's stupid. And I was beginning

to wonder about the idea of marrying an inmate by proxy. No bridesmaids, no bridegrooms, no music, no whisky, and no flowers. She convinced him to just sign on the dotted line. But then again, love makes you do extraordinary things. I ought to know: I been in love so many times when I hear my alarm clock go off in the morning it sounds like wedding bells.

The letter Roloff referred to would have had to be planted during the strip search, and I just can't accept that as an explanation. The very idea that someone planted that letter in Stephanie's bra just doesn't make sense to me, and it sounds pretty devious for her to assert that. Maybe Stephanie ain't so stupid after all.

May 15, 2006, 11:16 A.M.

Sheriff Smith,

I'm in Tyler occasionally to visit with Mrs. Toner, Stephanie's grandmother. Last weekend I went to the trailer where the Barrons were murdered. Everything is pretty much cleaned out with the exception of Stephanie's room. It's still the same as the day she left with pictures on the wall. The window in her mother's room is still broken from the shot that was fired. I needed to get some things Stephanie wanted me to have, so I made that walk next door. It was difficult for me to be in Stephanie's room for the first time.

I took flowers to the Barrons' graves. Looking at the markers with both saying, "December 25, 1999" made everything very real for me. My son and me left Tyler that afternoon, and neither of us spoke a word the entire way back to Rosenberg. The reality of it all left us in shock. I'd read the legal work and all the newspaper articles and had spent countless hours talking with Stephanie about that night. None of it became real for me until I stood in that house and then went to the cemetery. BTW Stephanie wants to talk to you.

Sincerely,
Steve Roloff

Holy shit. I'd been wondering if Rasco and I should go to Gatesville Prison and interview Stephanie Barron. I thought it might round out the book, so to speak. And here she says come on down with the possibility of new evidence. Prisoners don't have to talk to nobody if they don't want to. That's the law. So I called Senior Warden Rebecca Adams, and she said she'd fix us up for a date on Monday, June 5, 2006.

Rasco and I met at headquarters at eight o'clock that morning. The drive to Gatesville took less time than we thought. About two and a half hours. We were a little early for our noon meeting with Mrs. Barron-Roloff.

The Gatesville Prison is three miles north of town on Highway 36 in Coryell County. The unit, which employs about 750 people, was established in 1980 and houses nearly two thousand females. Stephanie is incarcerated in the Hilltop Unit, one of several in the Gatesville system. Following identification requirements at the administration building, Lieutenant

Woodlock, who has worked there since 1981, escorted us past the Trusty Camp and to the World War II-style reception center. Our interview room was a sparse, vacant office, but it was air conditioned. The state prison system isn't required to air condition any room, but my jail's temperature must fall between certain state-mandated guidelines.

Rasco read Stephanie her rights. She was dressed in white, all the way to her tennis shoes. She was shorter than I recall and prettier. She looked like she was ready to be picked up for a date. A little eyeliner, a little lip gloss. Her complexion was flawless, and her hands were well manicured. I remember actually thinking that prison life somehow agreed with her. I told Stephanie that her husband asked us to interview her because he believes she's innocent based on information we don't have.

Rasco looked her right in the eye. "As long as you don't have an attorney, we can talk. Do you have an attorney?"

"No, sir."

"Stephanie, can you tell us anything new about the night of the murders? Did you kill your parents?"

"No, sir, I did not."

"Then you're gonna have to convince us otherwise. If at any moment I think you're lying, we're gonna pack up right then and leave. Understand?"

"Yes, sir."

"What happened?"

206

# Epilogue

"What I didn't put in my original story was that on Christmas Eve I snuck out of the house to pick up Dinario. It was about 11:30. He came over a lot when my mom was not at home. My dad was never there; I had no relationship with him. And I couldn't really talk to my mom."

"Dinario had a gun that night?"

"He always had a gun."

"Had you seen this gun before?"

"Yes, sir."

"Had you fired that gun?"

"Yes, sir."

"Why did you fire the gun?"

"Dinario showed me how to shoot that summer. He wanted me to know how if I was gonna be his driver."

"What do you mean driver?"

"I drove him to his drug deals. We went to Dallas. We broke into a lake house once and sold some stuff."

"So you knew about his activity, but you didn't tell anyone?"

"Yes, sir."

"Stephanie, you lied to us and your attorneys. Why?"

"It was Dinario. He made me do it."

"You ruined your life because Dinario said so?"

"You don't understand."

"We understand all we know, Stephanie. You say you snuck out. Where were your parents?"

"Asleep. They never knew how many times I snuck out of the house. They trusted me."

"Then what happened that night?"

"I drove to Dinario's house. We rode around for a while, and then I brought him to my bedroom. The dogs didn't bark because they knew Dinario. We had sex. Then Dinario got up to go to the bathroom."

"What time was that?"

"Around three a.m. That was when I heard gunshots. I was terrified."

"Did you know Dinario had a gun that night?"

"Like I said, he always carried a gun."

"Dinario came back into my room and said, 'I just killed your mom and dad.' He left the gun on my bed, and I drove him back to his house."

"You didn't check on your parents?"

"No, sir. I panicked."

"What did you two say on the way to his house?"

"Nothing, really. He said he loved me."

"Now, Stephanie. That's a little hard to believe. You two didn't speak right after your parents had been murdered?

"Yes, sir. That's correct. I guess I was in shock."

"When you returned home, how did you know your parents were dead? Did you go into the bedroom? Did you look at your parents?"

"Yes, I went into their bedroom. The light was off. I couldn't look."

"They could have been alive, Stephanie. You could have helped them."

"I guess so. I wasn't thinking. I was in shock."

"Stephanie, did you and Dinario talk about killing your parents before this?"

"Yes, sir. Dinario talked about it a couple of times. In November, Mom was working on the computer in the next room, and he said he was going to kill her right then. I wouldn't let him."

"Did you take him seriously when he said he'd kill your parents?"

"Yes and no. I didn't think he'd really do it."

"Did you tell your parents this?"

"No, sir. I realize now I should have, but I was in a very abusive mental and physical relationship with Dinario. I was brain washed, but I loved him, and he loved me. That's what he said when I took him home, that he loved me. But he was sick."

"What do you mean sick?"

"He was very controlling. I realize that now."

"What else did he say to you?"

"To remain calm."

"Did you two plan to kill your parents the night of the murders?"

No, sir. There was no plan."

"What happened next? Did you go straight home after you dropped off Dinario?"

"Yes, sir. It took me seven minutes. Dinario used to time me and make me call him when I got home. He didn't give me any instructions, so I decided to make it look like someone came in and killed my parents. I cut the phone lines to the house and put the cutters in the bottom of the clothes hamper in the laundry room."

"That was your idea to make it look like there was an intruder?"

"Yes, sir. I wanted to make it look like someone robbed them, so I pulled out some drawers."

"Did you see your parents at that time?"

"No, sir. I couldn't look."

Rasco paused several seconds when we noticed Stephanie was crying as she recreated the night of the murders.

"Stephanie, why didn't you just tell the truth?"

"He said he'd kill me and my grandparents if I told anyone that he did it. I knew he would. He's been in lots of trouble, but I don't know if he's killed anyone else. Except those two in the house fire."

"You knew about the house fires and the deaths, but you didn't come forward and tell anyone?"

"That's correct. I knew."

"He threatened you, and that's why you lied to your attorneys?"

# Epilogue

"Yes, sir. He's psychotic. He manipulated me. And I didn't want to put my grandparents through a trial. They couldn't take it. He burned my car just to intimidate me. He's evil."

We were interviewing Barron-Roloff in a busy area on the second floor. I could hear the hum of office workers, Woodlock on his radio, and old air-conditioning units that hung from the ceilings. I sat across from Stephanie and listened to all this when two key words absolutely kicked my ass, words that have come up time and again in the book: *psychotic* and *manipulate*. Stephanie said Dinario came to the jail to see her every day until we put him in jail too. Maybe that was part of his plan: to keep Stephanie under his thumb by seeing her every day. I wanted to know how they hooked up and what in hell attracted her to Jones. So I asked her if they went to the same school.

"No, sir. He went to John Tyler High School. We met at the mall in Tyler in February 1997. I was working at Apple Fitness and attended school at night to get my GED. That's where I met my husband, Steve Roloff. He played racquetball. Dinario and I started dating in 1998. He was cool, and I was too rebellious for my own good."

I told her twice that if there was anything I needed to know, any physical evidence at all that would help clear her name, I would follow up. But she didn't really give me hard facts that I could use except one name, a person in prison who apparently heard Dinario admit to the murders, but that might not hold up in court. She also said that a male friend called her the night of the murder, and he was looking for Dinario. Apparently he knew Jones was there. Stephanie also said that her husband, Steve, had some letters written by Dinario that would incriminate him. I told Rasco to look into it.

"Stephanie," I asked, "what happened to you? You were Little Miss Perfect. Your grades were good. You weren't in trouble."

"I wasn't exactly perfect, especially after that terrible night in the motel where I got raped by three black guys. I was sixteen. That's when I lost my virginity. I smoked some marijuana that night. I found out later it was laced with embalming fluid. That guy's in the pen now for raping a fourteen-year-old girl and not registering as a sex offender. That's what started things going bad for me. But I never been pregnant and never had an abortion. My grades started dropping when my mom got a brain tumor. But like I said, I met Dinario. It was exciting. Drugs and alcohol. He sold crack."

Rasco continued. "Did you sell drugs?"

"No, sir. I just went with him. I was the driver."

"Stephanie, after the murders, you ran over to Grandma Toner's and called 911?"

"Yes, sir. I had nowhere else to go. I didn't kill my parents. I was young and stupid. I hate Dinario Jones for what he's done to me."

"Have you corresponded with Jones since you've been

here?"

"Yes, but not since 2003."

"We need those letters if they contain any information that will help you."

"Contact my husband. He's got them. I'll tell him it's OK to give them to you."

"You say that you knew sooner or later Dinario was going to kill your parents. Why?"

"Yes, I knew, but I didn't do anything about it. I should have. I think he was jealous and controlling, and he wanted the insurance money. He's an evil human being."

June 19, 2006, 10:51 a.m.
Sheriff Smith,

I did not go to Gatesville this Father's day weekend. I needed a break. These past few weeks of re-living all of this again has put a strain on me. As much as I love my wife, and as much as I believe in her innocence, the fact remains her parents were murdered as a result of the lifestyle she was living. That is a very difficult thing for me to swallow. It is overwhelming at times and I have to block it out of my mind or I would have a nervous breakdown. I spent Sunday with my parents and children. I needed a normal, relaxing day away from all the drama.

My marriage to Stephanie is what it is right now and may never change. Letters, yes, we write each other every day. Our visits, I see her every Sunday except when her grandma visits her. Other than that we look forward to the day when she will be home. When I first started corresponding with Stephanie I had no idea I would fall in love with her. Somewhere in the lines of her letters I realized I had fallen in love with this girl with my heart and soul. I understood there would be no sex, no candlelight dinners, or walks hand in hand on the beach. I know for the rest of my life I'll spend every Christmas Eve in a hotel waiting for visitation time on Christmas Day if it falls on a Sunday. Sheriff, I know that I could search high and low for the rest of my life and never find another woman that needs me as much as Stephanie does. After all, isn't that what love is all about? My joy comes from giving more than receiving. I do want my wife to come home, but my relationship with her is solid and I will stand by her even it if means twenty-three more years of prison. I am not a rich man by any means, but I will spend every dollar I ever make to see that she is released from that prison. Judge Gohmert said to Stephanie as she was led away to serve her seventy-five-year sentence that by the time she got out of prison her grandparents will be dead and she will be all alone. I guess I proved him wrong because Stephanie will never be alone again!

Sincerely,
Steve Roloff

If there's one thing I insist upon from my two boys, it's a call on Father's Day. I don't give a rip about birthdays, but

# Epilogue

Father's Day is a big deal for me because I never had my real father to be with. Roloff probably did the right thing by staying home with his family. I know about drama, and I need a break now and then too.

I wanted to read those letters written by Dinario Jones. We could match the handwriting to statements he wrote during interrogation. In my line of work, we're always careful about hearsay, and original letters are not considered hearsay. In a court of law, some statements are deemed hearsay because the person who initially made the statement isn't in the courtroom and can't be cross-examined. So that's where the rule of hearsay came from and why some spoken statements can't be admitted as evidence. And another thing: it's very possible that the statement hasn't been repeated accurately. Hell, the person who said something wasn't even under oath, so who knows about the accuracy of quoting a person who's in the pen. And finally, the right to confront witnesses is one of the mainstays of our legal system. We sure wanted to confront Dinario Jones, but we didn't think he'd talk to us. The only way to get an inmate to talk is to offer him something or get a court order based on compelling evidence.

Hope for a new trial for Stephanie Barron seemed out of the question to me. Stephanie Barron-Rollof's best shot was a cut in jail time if anything.

In a letter dated June 25, 2006, Roloff thanked me for taking the time to visit with Stephanie. I appreciate that. He also wrote that his wife was overwhelmed when she saw Detective Rasco and deeply regrets not trusting him at the time of the murders.

According to Roloff, Stephanie doesn't resemble the little girl I arrested in 1999 and deserves another chance at life because she was a confused girl who was involved with a dangerous young man. He asked in the interest of serving justice that I recommend and sponsor a time cut, because by law I can do that and because I was probably the most powerful man in Smith County. Hell, I knew that. He didn't want her to get out of prison at age fifty and live in a halfway house. I understand, but sponsoring anybody without new evidence ain't my job. It was a very good letter, but that's just not the way it works.

July 1, 2006
Sheriff Smith,

I appreciate your honesty and your position does not surprise me. I knew this wasn't going to be an easy task. Nonetheless, I intend to try and I intend to enlist the help of Detective Rasco as well, if he has time and if that's OK with you. I believe he is an honorable man. Who knows, maybe Detective Rasco will find that new evidence we need. I think if anyone could, it would be him. You have my permission to use my e-mails and you don't have to change my name. I used to be afraid for anyone to find out that I was married to Stephanie

Barron, but now I am proud of what she has done with herself while in jail.

Sincerely,
Steve Roloff

The Dinario Jones letters I requested finally arrived on Thursday, July 6. This guy's handwriting was so small I couldn't read it. My secretary, who is a retired schoolteacher, took one look at the handwriting and said there's something wrong with this person. People who write that small have something to hide.

Detective Rasco had to read the letters with a magnifying glass. Based on his perception of the letters, Rasco couldn't find anything that he considered incriminating evidence. He told me that Jones did respond to Stephanie's question about admitting guilt for committing the crimes. But the right words weren't there. It was too vague. Jones used the word *shit* for just about every noun he needed. At first Jones apparently didn't understand what Stephanie was asking, but then he wrote, "I can read between the lines, Shorty." He rarely called her Stephanie; he preferred "Lady" and "Shorty." He wrote that he would admit to murdering her parents if it would help her gain her freedom, but here's the way he said it: "Tell the people I'll take the case . . . if you want me to." He went on to write, "Hell, yeah, if they said here go kill the president and you and Shorty can be together. Man, I'd smoke that fool at point blank range then chop him up and set it on fire. Ha Ha Ha!!!" Rasco wasn't sure about the word *smoke*, but it wasn't *shoot*. Jones didn't use the words *murder* or *kill*.

It was obvious that Dinario still loved her. That was the theme throughout all of the letters that Rasco read. But as Stephanie began to withdraw from Dinario, he became more desperate to keep her as his wife. He considered Stephanie married to him and urged her to use his last name when signing her letters. Although I don't have her letters, it seems that she went along with that. They had decided to serve their terms together but apart, if that makes sense. He signed his letters, "Always yo husband."

I hope this sounds as familiar to you as it does to me. Instead of Jones manipulating Barron, it sounds the other way around. I think she was presenting herself as the victim of a controlling man. Much of this book's premise is based on the generally held idea that Dr. Wade French explained to me: psychopaths are experts at manipulation whenever they need anything. It sounds consistent to me that Stephanie Barron manipulated Dinario Jones and Steve Roloff. Maybe others too. That's one way inmates survive in the pen, and as I've said, Stephanie looked like incarceration agreed with her.

I'm signing off on this case because I got to get this book to press. I asked Detective Rasco to follow up on the people Stephanie Barron-Jones-Roloff mentioned in the interview. I'll continue to keep my mind open to any and all information

Epilogue

concerning this case, but I believe in my heart that Stephanie Barron is where she belongs.

And I got more books to write.

Seventeen-year-old Stephanie Barron, her
high school annual photo.

Carla and Stephen Barron.

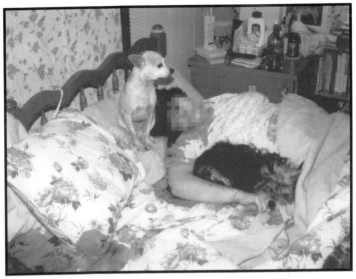

Christmas morning, 1999. The pet dogs stand guard
over Carla Barron.

Stephen Barron, who died as he reached for weapons under the bed.

Back view of the Barron home off County Road 219 in Chapel Hill.

Front view of the Barron home. Stephanie's bedroom is on the right.

Detective Joe Rasco, lead investigator on the Barron murder case.

The murder weapon, a Charter Arms .38 revolver.

Entrance to Stephanie Barron's bedroom.

Photo Date : 12/06/1999    Photo Time : 12:14am
SO#  : 94323    PID : 2132673

Name : BARRON, STEPHANIE CATHERINE    DOB : 05/08/1982

Sex  : F    Hgt : 500    Hair: BRO
Race : W    Wgt : 110    Eyes: GRN
Eth  : N

Build: S (SMALL)
Compl: LGT (LIGHT)

SMT  :

Stephanie Barron, the day she was arrested for forgery.

Photo Date : 01/14/2000    Photo Time : 09:48pm
SO# : 95094    PID : 2139136

Name : JONES, DINARIO THERRELL    DOB : 10/23/1982

Sex : M    Hgt : 509    Hair: BLK
Race : B    Wgt : 135    Eyes: BRO
Eth : N

Build: S (SMALL)
Compl: DRK (DARK)

SMT :

Dinario Jones, the day of his arrest for the arson of Stephanie's car.

Sheriff J. B. Smith.